50 Art of French Cooking Recipes for Home

By: Kelly Johnson

Table of Contents

- Beef Bourguignon
- Coq au Vin
- Ratatouille
- Croque Monsieur
- Bouillabaisse
- Quiche Lorraine
- Cassoulet
- Escargots (Snails in Garlic Butter)
- Duck à l'Orange
- Tarte Tatin (Upside-Down Apple Tart)
- Confit de Canard (Duck Confit)
- Sole Meunière
- Boeuf en Daube (Beef Stew)
- Salade Niçoise
- Crème Brûlée
- Pâté en Croûte (Pâté in Pastry)
- Soupe à l'Oignon (French Onion Soup)
- Steak Frites
- Profiteroles
- Coquilles Saint-Jacques (Scallops in Cream Sauce)
- Mousse au Chocolat
- Poulet à la Provençale (Provençal Chicken)
- Galette des Rois (King Cake)
- Gratin Dauphinois
- Navarin d'Agneau (Lamb Stew)
- Îles Flottantes (Floating Islands)
- Lapin à la Moutarde (Mustard Rabbit)
- Gougères (Cheese Puffs)
- Pain Perdu (French Toast)
- Pot-au-Feu (Beef Stew)
- Salade Lyonnaise
- Clafoutis (Cherry Flan)
- Rillettes de Porc (Pork Rillettes)
- Boucheés à la Reine (Vol-au-Vents)
- Boudin Blanc (White Sausage)
- Poulet Basquaise (Basque Chicken)

- Far Breton (Prune Cake)
- Brioche
- Pissaladière (Onion Tart)
- Madeleines
- Tartiflette (Potato, Reblochon Cheese, and Bacon Dish)
- Moules Marinières (Mussels in White Wine)
- Crêpes Suzette
- Blanquette de Veau (Veal Stew)
- Gratin de Pommes de Terre (Potato Gratin)
- Boeuf Bourguignon
- Normandy-style Chicken
- Piperade
- Navarin Printanier
- Strawberry Tart

Beef Bourguignon

Ingredients:

- 2 lbs (about 1 kg) beef chuck roast, cut into cubes
- 4 slices bacon, chopped
- 2 tablespoons all-purpose flour
- 2 tablespoons tomato paste
- 2 cups red wine (Burgundy wine is traditional)
- 2 cups beef broth
- 4 cloves garlic, minced
- 2 onions, chopped
- 4 carrots, sliced
- 1 bouquet garni (a bundle of herbs like thyme, parsley, and bay leaves tied together)
- Salt and pepper to taste
- Olive oil, as needed
- Chopped fresh parsley, for garnish

Instructions:

1. **Prepare the Beef:**
   - Pat dry the beef cubes with paper towels. Season generously with salt and pepper.
   - In a large Dutch oven or heavy-bottomed pot, heat a tablespoon of olive oil over medium-high heat.
   - Add the chopped bacon and cook until browned and crispy. Remove the bacon with a slotted spoon and set aside.
2. **Brown the Beef:**
   - In the same pot with the bacon drippings, add the beef cubes in batches (do not overcrowd the pot) and brown on all sides. Transfer the browned beef to a plate and set aside.
3. **Sauté the Vegetables:**
   - Add the chopped onions and sliced carrots to the pot. Sauté for about 5 minutes until softened and lightly browned.
   - Add the minced garlic and cook for another minute until fragrant.
4. **Deglaze the Pot:**
   - Sprinkle the flour over the vegetables and stir well to coat.
   - Add the tomato paste and stir for another minute.
   - Pour in the red wine and beef broth, stirring to scrape up any browned bits from the bottom of the pot.
5. **Simmer the Stew:**
   - Return the browned beef cubes and crispy bacon to the pot.
   - Add the bouquet garni (bundle of herbs) to the pot.

- Bring the mixture to a simmer, then reduce the heat to low. Cover the pot and let it simmer gently for 2 to 2 1/2 hours, or until the beef is tender and the sauce has thickened. Stir occasionally.
6. **Finish and Serve:**
    - Once the beef is tender, taste and adjust seasoning with salt and pepper if needed.
    - Discard the bouquet garni.
    - Serve Beef Bourguignon hot, garnished with chopped fresh parsley.

Serving Suggestions:

- Beef Bourguignon is traditionally served with crusty bread, mashed potatoes, or over buttered noodles to soak up the delicious sauce.
- Pair with a glass of red wine, such as Burgundy, to complement the flavors.

Enjoy this comforting and flavorful Beef Bourguignon, a staple of French cuisine that's perfect for special occasions or cozy family dinners!

Coq au Vin

Ingredients:

- 1 whole chicken (about 3-4 lbs), cut into pieces
- 4 ounces (115g) bacon, diced
- 12-15 pearl onions, peeled
- 2 cups red wine (Burgundy or Pinot Noir)
- 2 cups chicken broth
- 4 cloves garlic, minced
- 2 tablespoons tomato paste
- 2 tablespoons all-purpose flour
- 2 tablespoons unsalted butter
- 2 tablespoons olive oil
- 1 bouquet garni (a bundle of herbs like thyme, parsley, and bay leaves tied together)
- Salt and pepper to taste
- Chopped fresh parsley, for garnish

Instructions:

1. **Marinate the Chicken:**
    - In a large bowl, combine the chicken pieces with half of the red wine. Add the minced garlic and season generously with salt and pepper. Let marinate for at least 1 hour or preferably overnight in the refrigerator.
2. **Cook the Bacon and Vegetables:**
    - In a large Dutch oven or heavy-bottomed pot, heat the olive oil over medium heat.
    - Add the diced bacon and cook until browned and crispy. Remove the bacon with a slotted spoon and set aside.
    - In the same pot, add the pearl onions and cook until lightly browned and caramelized. Remove and set aside with the bacon.
3. **Brown the Chicken:**
    - Remove the chicken pieces from the marinade, reserving the marinade liquid.
    - Pat dry the chicken pieces with paper towels.
    - Heat the butter in the same pot over medium-high heat.
    - Working in batches, brown the chicken pieces on all sides until golden brown. Remove and set aside.
4. **Make the Sauce:**
    - Reduce the heat to medium and sprinkle the flour over the remaining fat in the pot. Cook, stirring constantly, for 1-2 minutes until the flour is lightly browned.
    - Add the tomato paste and stir for another minute.
    - Gradually add the remaining red wine and chicken broth, stirring constantly to combine and scrape up any browned bits from the bottom of the pot.
    - Return the chicken, bacon, and pearl onions to the pot.

- Add the bouquet garni (bundle of herbs) to the pot.
- Bring the mixture to a simmer, then reduce the heat to low. Cover the pot and let it simmer gently for 1 to 1 1/2 hours, or until the chicken is tender and cooked through.

5. **Finish and Serve:**
    - Once the chicken is cooked through, taste and adjust seasoning with salt and pepper if needed.
    - Discard the bouquet garni.
    - Serve Coq au Vin hot, garnished with chopped fresh parsley.

Serving Suggestions:

- Coq au Vin is traditionally served with crusty bread, mashed potatoes, or over buttered noodles to soak up the delicious sauce.
- Pair with a glass of red wine, such as Burgundy or Pinot Noir, to complement the flavors.

Enjoy this classic French dish, Coq au Vin, which brings together the robust flavors of chicken, wine, and herbs for a comforting and satisfying meal!

Ratatouille

Ingredients:

- 1 large eggplant, diced
- 2 medium zucchinis, diced
- 1 large bell pepper (red or yellow), diced
- 2 medium tomatoes, diced
- 1 onion, finely chopped
- 4 cloves garlic, minced
- 1/4 cup olive oil
- 1 tablespoon tomato paste
- 1 teaspoon dried thyme (or 1 tablespoon fresh thyme leaves)
- 1 teaspoon dried oregano (or 1 tablespoon fresh oregano leaves)
- Salt and pepper to taste
- Fresh basil leaves, thinly sliced, for garnish

Instructions:

1. **Prepare the Vegetables:**
   - Heat 2 tablespoons of olive oil in a large skillet or Dutch oven over medium heat.
   - Add the diced eggplant and cook for 5-7 minutes, stirring occasionally, until softened and lightly browned. Remove from the skillet and set aside.
2. **Cook the Onions and Garlic:**
   - In the same skillet, add the remaining olive oil.
   - Add the chopped onion and cook for 3-4 minutes until translucent.
   - Add the minced garlic and cook for another minute until fragrant.
3. **Combine the Vegetables:**
   - Add the diced zucchini and bell pepper to the skillet with the onions and garlic. Cook for 5-6 minutes until the vegetables start to soften.
4. **Add Tomatoes and Tomato Paste:**
   - Stir in the diced tomatoes and tomato paste. Cook for 3-4 minutes until the tomatoes begin to break down and release their juices.
5. **Simmer the Ratatouille:**
   - Return the cooked eggplant to the skillet.
   - Stir in the dried thyme, dried oregano, salt, and pepper to taste.
   - Reduce the heat to low, cover the skillet, and let the ratatouille simmer for 20-25 minutes, stirring occasionally, until all the vegetables are tender and flavors are well combined.
6. **Finish and Serve:**
   - Taste and adjust seasoning if needed.
   - Garnish with thinly sliced fresh basil leaves before serving.

Serving Suggestions:

- Ratatouille can be served warm or at room temperature.
- It pairs well with crusty bread, rice, pasta, or even as a side dish to grilled meats or fish.
- Drizzle with a little extra olive oil and sprinkle with additional fresh herbs before serving for extra flavor.

Enjoy this colorful and flavorful Ratatouille, a delicious taste of Provence that's perfect for showcasing summer vegetables!

Croque Monsieur

Ingredients:

- 8 slices of bread (traditionally pain de mie or brioche)
- 8 slices of ham
- 8 slices of Gruyère cheese (or Emmental cheese)
- Butter, softened, for spreading

For the Béchamel Sauce:

- 2 tablespoons unsalted butter
- 2 tablespoons all-purpose flour
- 1 cup milk
- Salt, pepper, and nutmeg to taste
- 1/2 cup grated Gruyère cheese (optional, for topping)

Instructions:

1. **Prepare the Béchamel Sauce:**
   - In a small saucepan, melt the butter over medium heat.
   - Stir in the flour and cook for about 1-2 minutes, stirring constantly, until it forms a paste (roux).
   - Gradually whisk in the milk, a little at a time, until smooth and thickened.
   - Season with salt, pepper, and a pinch of nutmeg. Cook for another 2-3 minutes until the sauce coats the back of a spoon.
   - Remove from heat and set aside.
2. **Assemble the Croque Monsieur:**
   - Preheat your oven to 400°F (200°C).
   - Lay out 4 slices of bread on a baking sheet lined with parchment paper.
   - Spread a layer of béchamel sauce on each slice of bread.
   - Place a slice of ham and a slice of Gruyère cheese on top of the béchamel sauce.
   - Place another slice of bread on top to form a sandwich.
   - Spread a thin layer of softened butter on the top slice of each sandwich.
3. **Bake the Croque Monsieur:**
   - Bake in the preheated oven for about 5-7 minutes, or until the tops are golden brown and the cheese is melted.
4. **Optional: Finish Under the Grill (Broiler):**
   - If desired, after baking, you can place the sandwiches under a preheated grill (broiler) for a minute or two to further brown and crisp up the tops.
5. **Serve:**
   - Remove from the oven (or grill) and let cool for a minute or two.
   - Optionally, sprinkle grated Gruyère cheese on top of each sandwich before serving for an extra cheesy crust.

    - Serve hot, optionally with a side of salad or pickles.

Tips:

- **Variations:** You can also make a Croque Madame by topping the Croque Monsieur with a fried or poached egg.
- **Bread:** If you can't find pain de mie or brioche, any good quality sandwich bread will work.
- **Cheese:** Feel free to experiment with different cheeses, but Gruyère or Emmental are traditional choices for their melting properties and flavor.

Enjoy this indulgent and comforting French sandwich, Croque Monsieur, perfect for a satisfying lunch or brunch option!

Bouillabaisse

Ingredients:

- 1 lb (450g) mixed seafood (such as shrimp, mussels, clams, firm white fish fillets like cod or halibut, scallops)
- 1 onion, chopped
- 2 cloves garlic, minced
- 1 fennel bulb, thinly sliced
- 1 leek, thinly sliced (white and light green parts only)
- 1 celery stalk, chopped
- 1 carrot, chopped
- 1 can (14 oz / 400g) diced tomatoes
- 4 cups fish or seafood stock
- 1 cup dry white wine
- 1/4 cup Pernod or other anise-flavored liqueur (optional)
- 2 tablespoons tomato paste
- 2 tablespoons olive oil
- 1 bay leaf
- 1 teaspoon saffron threads
- Salt and pepper to taste
- Fresh parsley, chopped, for garnish
- Crusty bread, for serving

Instructions:

1. **Prepare the Seafood:**
   - Clean and prepare the seafood as needed. Peel and devein shrimp if necessary. Scrub mussels and clams under cold water. Cut fish fillets into bite-sized pieces.
2. **Sauté Aromatics:**
   - Heat olive oil in a large pot or Dutch oven over medium heat.
   - Add chopped onion, garlic, fennel, leek, celery, and carrot. Sauté for 5-7 minutes until vegetables are softened.
3. **Add Tomatoes and Tomato Paste:**
   - Stir in tomato paste and cook for 1-2 minutes.
   - Add diced tomatoes (with juices) and cook for another 5 minutes, stirring occasionally.
4. **Add Liquids and Seasonings:**
   - Pour in white wine and Pernod (if using). Bring to a simmer and cook for 5 minutes to reduce slightly.
   - Add fish or seafood stock, bay leaf, saffron threads, salt, and pepper. Bring to a boil, then reduce heat to low. Cover and simmer for 20-25 minutes to develop flavors.
5. **Add Seafood:**

- Start with the seafood that takes the longest to cook (such as firm fish) and add it to the pot. Simmer for a few minutes.
- Add remaining seafood (shrimp, mussels, clams, scallops) and continue to simmer for another 5-7 minutes until all seafood is cooked through and mussels and clams have opened. Discard any that do not open.

6. **Serve:**
    - Remove bay leaf from the pot.
    - Ladle Bouillabaisse into bowls, making sure to distribute seafood evenly.
    - Garnish with chopped fresh parsley.
    - Serve hot with crusty bread for dipping into the flavorful broth.

Tips:

- **Variations:** Bouillabaisse traditionally includes a variety of seafood, but you can adjust the types of seafood based on availability and preference.
- **Bread:** Serve with rouille (a garlic saffron mayonnaise) and crusty bread for a classic accompaniment.

Enjoy this hearty and aromatic Bouillabaisse, a taste of the Mediterranean that's perfect for a special occasion or cozy dinner at home!

Quiche Lorraine

Ingredients:

- 1 pie crust (homemade or store-bought), chilled
- 6 ounces (170g) bacon or lardons, diced
- 1 cup shredded Gruyère cheese (or Swiss cheese)
- 4 large eggs
- 1 cup heavy cream
- 1/2 cup whole milk
- 1/4 teaspoon salt
- 1/4 teaspoon black pepper
- 1/4 teaspoon ground nutmeg
- 1 tablespoon unsalted butter, melted

Instructions:

1. **Preheat the Oven:**
   - Preheat your oven to 375°F (190°C).
2. **Prepare the Pie Crust:**
   - Roll out the pie crust and fit it into a 9-inch tart pan or pie dish. Trim any excess dough and crimp the edges. Prick the bottom of the crust with a fork. Chill the crust in the refrigerator while you prepare the filling.
3. **Cook the Bacon:**
   - In a skillet over medium heat, cook the diced bacon until crispy. Remove from the skillet and drain on paper towels.
4. **Prepare the Custard Filling:**
   - In a bowl, whisk together the eggs, heavy cream, milk, salt, pepper, and nutmeg until well combined.
5. **Assemble the Quiche:**
   - Sprinkle half of the shredded cheese and cooked bacon evenly over the bottom of the chilled pie crust.
   - Pour the egg mixture over the bacon and cheese in the pie crust.
   - Sprinkle the remaining cheese on top.
6. **Bake the Quiche:**
   - Place the quiche on a baking sheet (to catch any drips) and bake in the preheated oven for 35-40 minutes, or until the quiche is set and golden brown on top.
7. **Finish and Serve:**
   - Remove from the oven and let the quiche cool slightly before slicing.
   - Brush the melted butter over the top of the quiche for a shiny finish (optional).
   - Serve warm or at room temperature.

Tips:

- **Variations:** You can add caramelized onions, spinach, mushrooms, or herbs to customize your Quiche Lorraine.
- **Make Ahead:** Quiche Lorraine can be baked ahead of time and reheated before serving. It's also delicious served cold.
- **Serving Suggestions:** Serve Quiche Lorraine with a side salad for a complete meal, or enjoy it as a savory brunch dish.

Enjoy this classic French dish, Quiche Lorraine, with its creamy filling, savory bacon, and cheese flavors encased in a crisp pie crust!

Cassoulet

Ingredients:

- 1 lb (450g) dried white beans (such as Great Northern beans or cannellini beans)
- 1 lb (450g) pork sausages (such as Toulouse sausages), cut into chunks
- 4 duck legs confit (or substitute with duck breasts)
- 1/2 lb (225g) pork belly, cut into chunks
- 1 onion, chopped
- 2 carrots, chopped
- 2 celery stalks, chopped
- 4 cloves garlic, minced
- 2 tablespoons tomato paste
- 2 cups chicken broth
- 2 cups beef broth
- 1 cup dry white wine
- 2 bay leaves
- 2 sprigs fresh thyme
- Salt and pepper to taste
- Bread crumbs, for topping
- Chopped fresh parsley, for garnish

Instructions:

1. **Prepare the Beans:**
   - Rinse the dried white beans under cold water. Place them in a large bowl and cover with cold water. Let soak overnight, or use the quick soak method by boiling them for 2 minutes and then letting them sit for 1 hour off the heat. Drain and set aside.
2. **Cook the Meats:**
   - Preheat your oven to 325°F (160°C).
   - In a large Dutch oven or heavy-bottomed pot, heat some olive oil over medium-high heat.
   - Brown the pork sausages, duck legs (if using raw), and pork belly in batches until golden brown on all sides. Remove and set aside.
3. **Sauté Aromatics:**
   - In the same pot, add chopped onion, carrots, and celery. Sauté for about 5 minutes until softened.
   - Add minced garlic and cook for another minute until fragrant.
4. **Add Tomato Paste and Liquids:**
   - Stir in tomato paste and cook for 1-2 minutes.
   - Pour in chicken broth, beef broth, and white wine. Stir to combine and scrape up any browned bits from the bottom of the pot.
5. **Simmer and Assemble:**

- Add the browned meats (sausages, duck confit, pork belly) back into the pot.
- Stir in drained beans, bay leaves, and fresh thyme sprigs.
- Bring the mixture to a simmer, then cover the pot and transfer to the preheated oven.

6. **Bake the Cassoulet:**
    - Bake uncovered for 2 to 2 1/2 hours, stirring occasionally, until the beans and meats are tender and the liquid has reduced to a thick stew consistency. If the top starts to brown too quickly, cover loosely with foil.
7. **Finish and Serve:**
    - Remove the Cassoulet from the oven and discard bay leaves and thyme sprigs.
    - Sprinkle bread crumbs evenly over the top of the Cassoulet.
    - Increase oven temperature to 400°F (200°C) and bake for an additional 15-20 minutes until the bread crumbs are golden brown and crispy.
8. **Garnish and Serve:**
    - Let the Cassoulet rest for a few minutes before serving.
    - Garnish with chopped fresh parsley and serve hot, preferably with crusty bread and a green salad.

Tips:

- **Meat Variations:** Feel free to customize your Cassoulet with different meats based on availability and preference, such as lamb shoulder, ham hock, or even chicken thighs.
- **Make Ahead:** Cassoulet tastes even better the next day after flavors have melded together. It can be stored in the refrigerator for several days and reheated gently.
- **Wine Pairing:** Serve Cassoulet with a robust red wine, such as a Bordeaux or a Syrah, to complement its rich flavors.

Enjoy this comforting and satisfying French dish, Cassoulet, which brings together tender beans, savory meats, and aromatic vegetables in a delightful stew!

Escargots (Snails in Garlic Butter)

Ingredients:

- 24 canned or frozen escargots (snails), rinsed and drained
- 24 snail shells (if not using pre-filled shells)
- 1/2 cup unsalted butter, softened
- 4 cloves garlic, minced
- 2 tablespoons fresh parsley, finely chopped
- 1 tablespoon shallot, finely minced (optional)
- 1 tablespoon white wine
- Salt and freshly ground black pepper, to taste
- Baguette or crusty bread, for serving

Instructions:

1. **Prepare the Escargots:**
   - If using canned or frozen escargots, rinse them thoroughly under cold water and drain well. If they're not already in shells, place each escargot into a clean snail shell.
2. **Make Garlic Butter:**
   - In a small bowl, combine softened butter, minced garlic, parsley, shallot (if using), white wine, salt, and pepper. Mix well until all ingredients are evenly incorporated.
3. **Assemble and Bake:**
   - Preheat your oven to 400°F (200°C).
   - Place each prepared escargot shell (with escargot inside) in a special escargot dish or on a baking dish with indentations to hold them upright.
   - Spoon a small amount of the garlic butter mixture over each escargot, filling the shell but not overflowing.
4. **Bake the Escargots:**
   - Bake in the preheated oven for 10-12 minutes, or until the butter is bubbling and the escargots are heated through.
5. **Serve:**
   - Remove from the oven and let cool slightly.
   - Serve immediately, preferably with slices of baguette or crusty bread for dipping into the garlic butter.

Tips:

- **Escargot Shells:** If you don't have special escargot dishes, you can use a mini muffin tin or any oven-safe dish with small indentations to hold the shells upright.
- **Wine Pairing:** Escargots pair wonderfully with a dry white wine, such as Chardonnay or Sauvignon Blanc, to complement the garlic butter and delicate flavors.

- **Variations:** Some recipes also include a pinch of ground nutmeg or a splash of cognac in the garlic butter mixture for added depth of flavor.

Enjoy this luxurious French appetizer, Escargots à la Bourguignonne, with its rich garlic butter sauce and tender snails served piping hot!

Duck à l'Orange

Ingredients:

- 2 duck breasts, skin-on
- Salt and pepper, to taste
- 1 tablespoon olive oil
- 1 tablespoon butter

For the Orange Sauce:

- 1 cup freshly squeezed orange juice (about 3-4 oranges)
- Zest of 1 orange
- 1/2 cup chicken or duck broth
- 1/4 cup dry white wine or Cognac
- 2 tablespoons honey or sugar
- 2 tablespoons red wine vinegar or balsamic vinegar
- 2 tablespoons unsalted butter, chilled
- Salt and pepper, to taste

Optional Garnish:

- Fresh thyme or parsley, chopped
- Orange slices or zest, for garnish

Instructions:

1. **Prepare the Duck Breasts:**
    - Pat the duck breasts dry with paper towels.
    - Score the duck skin in a crosshatch pattern, being careful not to cut into the meat. This helps render the fat and crisp up the skin.
    - Season both sides of the duck breasts with salt and pepper.
2. **Cook the Duck Breasts:**
    - Heat olive oil and butter in a large skillet over medium-high heat.
    - Place the duck breasts in the skillet, skin-side down. Cook for about 5-7 minutes, or until the skin is golden brown and crispy. Turn the breasts over and cook for another 3-5 minutes for medium-rare, or longer to desired doneness. Remove from the skillet and let rest on a cutting board.
3. **Make the Orange Sauce:**
    - In the same skillet, pour off excess fat, leaving about 1-2 tablespoons.
    - Add orange juice, orange zest, chicken broth, white wine or Cognac, honey or sugar, and red wine vinegar or balsamic vinegar to the skillet. Bring to a simmer over medium heat, scraping up any browned bits from the bottom of the skillet.
    - Simmer until the sauce is reduced by half and slightly thickened, about 10-15 minutes.

4. **Finish the Sauce:**
   - Remove the skillet from heat and whisk in chilled butter, one tablespoon at a time, until incorporated and the sauce is glossy. Season with salt and pepper to taste.
5. **Slice and Serve:**
   - Slice the duck breasts diagonally into thin slices.
   - Arrange the duck slices on serving plates and spoon the orange sauce over the top.
   - Garnish with chopped fresh thyme or parsley and orange slices or zest, if desired.

Tips:

- **Resting Time:** Letting the duck breasts rest after cooking allows the juices to redistribute, resulting in juicier meat.
- **Serving Suggestions:** Duck à l'Orange pairs well with roasted potatoes, wild rice, or a simple green salad.
- **Wine Pairing:** Serve with a medium-bodied red wine like Pinot Noir or a fruity white wine such as Riesling to complement the flavors of the dish.

Enjoy this elegant and flavorful Duck à l'Orange, a classic French dish that beautifully balances savory duck with the bright acidity of oranges!

Tarte Tatin (Upside-Down Apple Tart)

Ingredients:

For the Pastry:

- 1 1/4 cups (160g) all-purpose flour
- 1/2 cup (113g) unsalted butter, cold and diced
- 1/4 cup (50g) granulated sugar
- 1/4 teaspoon salt
- 2-3 tablespoons ice water

For the Apple Filling:

- 6-8 apples (such as Granny Smith or Golden Delicious), peeled, cored, and halved
- 1/2 cup (100g) granulated sugar
- 1/4 cup (55g) unsalted butter
- 1 tablespoon lemon juice
- 1/2 teaspoon ground cinnamon (optional)

Instructions:

1. **Prepare the Pastry:**
    - In a large bowl, combine the flour, sugar, and salt.
    - Add the cold diced butter and quickly rub or cut it into the flour mixture using your fingertips or a pastry cutter until it resembles coarse crumbs.
    - Gradually add ice water, 1 tablespoon at a time, and mix until the dough comes together. Form the dough into a ball, flatten it into a disk, wrap in plastic wrap, and refrigerate for at least 30 minutes.
2. **Prepare the Apple Filling:**
    - Preheat your oven to 375°F (190°C).
    - In a 9-inch (23cm) oven-safe skillet or Tarte Tatin pan, melt the butter over medium heat.
    - Stir in the granulated sugar and cook, stirring constantly, until the sugar is dissolved and turns golden brown, about 5-7 minutes. Be careful not to burn the caramel.
    - Remove the skillet from heat and carefully arrange the apple halves, rounded side down, in a circular pattern over the caramel. Fill any gaps with smaller pieces of apple.
    - Sprinkle lemon juice and cinnamon (if using) evenly over the apples.
3. **Assemble and Bake:**
    - On a lightly floured surface, roll out the chilled pastry dough into a circle slightly larger than the skillet.
    - Carefully place the pastry over the apples, tucking the edges down around the apples to encase them.

- Pierce the pastry with a fork in several places to allow steam to escape.
- Bake in the preheated oven for 30-35 minutes, or until the pastry is golden brown and crisp.

4. **Invert and Serve:**
    - Remove the Tarte Tatin from the oven and let it cool in the skillet for 5-10 minutes.
    - Place a serving plate over the skillet and, using oven mitts, carefully invert the Tarte Tatin onto the plate. Be cautious as the caramel may be hot and sticky.
    - Serve warm or at room temperature. Optionally, garnish with whipped cream, vanilla ice cream, or a dusting of powdered sugar.

Tips:

- **Choosing Apples:** Use firm apples that hold their shape well when cooked, such as Granny Smith or Golden Delicious.
- **Caramel:** Be attentive when making the caramel to avoid burning it. Stir constantly until the sugar is fully dissolved and turns a deep golden brown.
- **Pastry Dough:** Keep the pastry dough chilled until ready to use to ensure it stays firm and easy to work with.

Enjoy this delightful and classic French dessert, Tarte Tatin, with its tender caramelized apples and buttery pastry, perfect for any occasion!

Confit de Canard (Duck Confit)

Ingredients:

- 4 duck legs, preferably with thighs attached
- 4 cups duck fat (or substitute with a mixture of duck fat and vegetable oil)
- 4 cloves garlic, smashed
- 4 sprigs fresh thyme
- 2 bay leaves
- Salt and freshly ground black pepper

Instructions:

1. **Prepare the Duck Legs:**
   - Pat the duck legs dry with paper towels and season generously with salt and pepper on both sides.
2. **Marinate:**
   - Place the duck legs in a shallow dish or large resealable plastic bag.
   - Add smashed garlic cloves, thyme sprigs, and bay leaves to the dish or bag, distributing them evenly around the duck legs.
   - Cover or seal the bag and refrigerate for at least 12 hours, preferably overnight, to allow the flavors to meld.
3. **Cooking:**
   - Preheat your oven to 225°F (110°C).
   - In a large, oven-safe pot or Dutch oven, melt the duck fat over low heat until it becomes liquid.
   - Remove the duck legs from the marinade, scraping off any excess herbs and garlic. Pat them dry with paper towels.
   - Arrange the duck legs in the pot in a single layer, skin-side down.
   - Pour the melted duck fat over the duck legs, making sure they are completely submerged. Add more fat or oil if needed.
   - Place the pot in the preheated oven and cook uncovered for about 2 1/2 to 3 hours, or until the duck is very tender and the meat starts to pull away from the bones.
4. **Cool and Store:**
   - Remove the pot from the oven and let the duck legs cool slightly in the fat.
   - Once cooled, transfer the duck legs along with the fat into sterilized jars or containers, making sure the duck legs are fully submerged in the fat. Seal tightly.
5. **Serve:**
   - Confit de Canard can be stored in the refrigerator for several weeks. To serve, gently reheat the duck legs in a skillet over medium-low heat until the skin is crispy and the meat is heated through.
   - Serve hot, accompanied by roasted potatoes, a green salad, or crusty bread.

Tips:

- **Rendering Fat:** Save the rendered duck fat after cooking the confit. It can be strained and reused for cooking other dishes, such as roasted potatoes or sautéed vegetables.
- **Crispy Skin:** For crispy skin, you can briefly pan-fry the duck legs, skin-side down, in a hot skillet before serving.
- **Storage:** Store the confit in the refrigerator for longer shelf life, or freeze for several months. Thaw overnight in the refrigerator before reheating.

Enjoy this luxurious and flavorful French dish, Duck Confit, with its tender, melt-in-your-mouth meat and rich, savory flavors!

Sole Meunière

Ingredients:

- 4 sole fillets (about 6-8 ounces each), skinless
- Salt and pepper, to taste
- All-purpose flour, for dredging
- 6 tablespoons unsalted butter, divided
- 2 tablespoons olive oil
- Juice of 1 lemon
- 2 tablespoons chopped fresh parsley, for garnish

Instructions:

1. **Prepare the Sole:**
   - Pat the sole fillets dry with paper towels. Season both sides with salt and pepper.
2. **Dredge in Flour:**
   - Dredge each sole fillet lightly in flour, shaking off any excess. This helps create a light coating for frying.
3. **Cook the Sole:**
   - In a large skillet, heat 3 tablespoons of butter and 2 tablespoons of olive oil over medium-high heat until the butter starts to foam.
   - Carefully place the sole fillets in the skillet, in batches if necessary to avoid overcrowding. Cook for about 2-3 minutes on each side, or until the fish is golden brown and cooked through. The cooking time will depend on the thickness of the fillets.
   - Transfer the cooked sole fillets to a plate and keep warm while you prepare the sauce.
4. **Make the Sauce:**
   - Reduce the heat to medium-low. Add the remaining 3 tablespoons of butter to the skillet. Allow it to melt and start to brown slightly, swirling the pan occasionally.
   - Once the butter is lightly browned and has a nutty aroma, remove the skillet from heat.
   - Carefully add the lemon juice to the browned butter (be cautious as it may sizzle). Swirl the skillet gently to combine the lemon juice with the butter.
5. **Serve:**
   - Pour the lemon butter sauce over the cooked sole fillets.
   - Garnish with chopped fresh parsley.

Tips:

- **Choosing Sole:** Use fresh sole fillets for the best flavor and texture. You can also use other delicate white fish fillets such as flounder or trout.

- **Brown Butter:** Cooking the butter until it browns slightly adds a nutty flavor to the sauce, enhancing the overall taste of the dish.
- **Garnish:** Fresh parsley adds a pop of color and freshness to the dish. You can also add a slice of lemon for additional garnish and flavor.

Serve Sole Meunière immediately while hot, accompanied by steamed vegetables, roasted potatoes, or a simple green salad. This elegant French dish is perfect for a special dinner or any occasion when you want to impress with classic flavors and techniques.

Boeuf en Daube (Beef Stew)

Ingredients:

- 2 lbs (about 1 kg) beef chuck or stewing beef, cut into 2-inch cubes
- Salt and freshly ground black pepper
- 4 tablespoons all-purpose flour
- 4 tablespoons olive oil, divided
- 4 ounces (115g) pancetta or bacon, diced
- 2 onions, diced
- 2 carrots, diced
- 2 celery stalks, diced
- 4 cloves garlic, minced
- 2 tablespoons tomato paste
- 2 cups red wine (such as Burgundy or Cabernet Sauvignon)
- 1 cup beef broth
- 2 bay leaves
- 1 sprig fresh thyme
- 1 sprig fresh rosemary
- 1 teaspoon dried Herbes de Provence (or a mixture of dried herbs like thyme, rosemary, marjoram)
- 1 tablespoon butter
- Chopped fresh parsley, for garnish

Instructions:

1. **Prepare the Beef:**
   - Season the beef cubes with salt and pepper. Dredge them in flour, shaking off any excess.
2. **Brown the Beef:**
   - In a large Dutch oven or heavy-bottomed pot, heat 2 tablespoons of olive oil over medium-high heat.
   - Add the beef cubes in batches and brown them on all sides, about 4-5 minutes per batch. Transfer the browned beef to a plate and set aside.
3. **Cook the Pancetta and Vegetables:**
   - In the same pot, add the diced pancetta or bacon. Cook until browned and crispy, stirring occasionally. Remove the pancetta with a slotted spoon and set aside.
   - Add the remaining 2 tablespoons of olive oil to the pot. Add diced onions, carrots, and celery. Cook, stirring occasionally, until the vegetables are softened, about 5-7 minutes.
   - Add minced garlic and cook for another 1-2 minutes until fragrant.
4. **Combine and Simmer:**
   - Stir in tomato paste and cook for 1-2 minutes.
   - Return the browned beef and cooked pancetta to the pot.

- Pour in red wine and beef broth, stirring to combine and scraping up any browned bits from the bottom of the pot.
- Add bay leaves, fresh thyme, rosemary, and dried Herbes de Provence. Season with salt and pepper to taste.

5. **Braise the Beef:**
   - Bring the mixture to a simmer. Cover the pot with a lid, leaving it slightly ajar.
   - Reduce the heat to low and let the stew simmer gently for 2 1/2 to 3 hours, stirring occasionally, until the beef is tender and the flavors have melded together.

6. **Finish and Serve:**
   - Remove the pot from heat. Discard the bay leaves, thyme sprig, and rosemary sprig.
   - Stir in 1 tablespoon of butter to enrich the sauce.
   - Taste and adjust seasoning with salt and pepper if needed.
   - Garnish with chopped fresh parsley before serving.

Serving Suggestions:

- Boeuf en Daube is traditionally served with crusty bread, mashed potatoes, or over buttered noodles to soak up the flavorful sauce.
- Pair with a glass of red wine, such as the same wine used in the stew, to complement the rich flavors.

Enjoy this hearty and comforting French beef stew, Boeuf en Daube, which is perfect for a cozy dinner with family or friends!

Salade Niçoise

Ingredients:

- 1 lb (450g) small new potatoes, halved or quartered
- 4 large eggs
- 1 lb (450g) fresh green beans, trimmed
- 1 pint (about 250g) cherry tomatoes, halved
- 1/2 cup Niçoise olives, pitted
- 2 (5-ounce) cans tuna, drained (preferably packed in olive oil)
- 4-6 anchovy fillets, optional
- 4 cups mixed salad greens (such as butter lettuce, arugula, or mesclun)
- 1/4 cup red onion, thinly sliced
- 2 tablespoons capers, drained

For the Vinaigrette:

- 1/4 cup extra-virgin olive oil
- 2 tablespoons red wine vinegar
- 1 tablespoon Dijon mustard
- 1 garlic clove, minced
- Salt and freshly ground black pepper, to taste

Instructions:

1. **Prepare the Eggs and Potatoes:**
   - Place the eggs in a saucepan and cover with cold water. Bring to a boil over high heat. Once boiling, reduce heat to medium-high and cook for 8-10 minutes for hard-boiled eggs. Transfer eggs to a bowl of ice water to cool. Peel and quarter the eggs.
   - In the same saucepan, cook the potatoes in salted boiling water until tender, about 10-15 minutes. Drain and let cool slightly.
2. **Blanch the Green Beans:**
   - In a separate pot of boiling salted water, blanch the green beans until crisp-tender, about 3-4 minutes. Drain and immediately transfer to a bowl of ice water to stop cooking. Drain again.
3. **Assemble the Salad:**
   - In a large salad bowl or on individual plates, arrange the mixed salad greens.
   - Arrange the cooked potatoes, blanched green beans, cherry tomatoes, Niçoise olives, tuna, anchovy fillets (if using), sliced red onion, quartered eggs, and capers over the greens in sections or in a pleasing arrangement.
4. **Make the Vinaigrette:**
   - In a small bowl, whisk together the olive oil, red wine vinegar, Dijon mustard, minced garlic, salt, and pepper until well combined.
5. **Serve:**

- - Drizzle the vinaigrette over the salad just before serving.
  - Optionally, garnish with additional fresh herbs like parsley or basil.

Tips:

- **Tuna:** Use high-quality canned tuna packed in olive oil for the best flavor.
- **Variations:** Traditional Salade Niçoise does not include cooked vegetables like potatoes and green beans, but these additions are commonly accepted variations.
- **Presentation:** Arrange the ingredients neatly on a platter or individual plates for an attractive presentation.

Salade Niçoise makes a satisfying main course salad, perfect for lunch or a light dinner, especially on warm days. It's versatile and can be customized to suit your taste preferences while still maintaining its classic Mediterranean flavors.

Crème Brûlée

Ingredients:

- 1 quart (4 cups) heavy cream
- 1 vanilla bean, split lengthwise and seeds scraped out (or 1 tablespoon pure vanilla extract)
- 8 large egg yolks
- 2/3 cup granulated sugar, plus extra for caramelizing
- Pinch of salt

Instructions:

1. **Preheat the Oven:**
   - Preheat your oven to 325°F (160°C). Place a large roasting pan filled with water on the bottom rack of the oven. This will create a water bath (bain-marie) to help the custards cook gently and evenly.
2. **Prepare the Cream Mixture:**
   - In a medium saucepan, combine the heavy cream and vanilla bean seeds (or vanilla extract). Heat over medium-high heat until it just begins to simmer. Remove from heat and let it steep for about 15 minutes to infuse the cream with vanilla flavor. Remove the vanilla bean pod if used.
3. **Whisk Egg Yolks and Sugar:**
   - In a large mixing bowl, whisk together the egg yolks, granulated sugar, and a pinch of salt until well combined and slightly thickened.
4. **Temper the Eggs:**
   - Gradually pour the warm cream mixture into the egg yolk mixture, whisking constantly, until well combined. This process is called tempering and prevents the eggs from scrambling.
5. **Strain the Mixture:**
   - Strain the custard mixture through a fine-mesh sieve into a large measuring cup or bowl with a spout. This step helps remove any bits of cooked egg or vanilla bean for a smooth texture.
6. **Fill Ramekins:**
   - Place six 6-ounce ramekins (or custard cups) in a baking dish or roasting pan. Divide the custard mixture evenly among the ramekins.
7. **Bake the Custards:**
   - Carefully pour hot water into the baking dish around the ramekins, about halfway up the sides of the ramekins, to create the water bath.
   - Bake in the preheated oven for 30-35 minutes, or until the custards are set around the edges but still slightly jiggly in the center. The cooking time may vary depending on your oven and the size of your ramekins.
8. **Chill the Custards:**

- Remove the ramekins from the water bath and let them cool to room temperature. Then cover each ramekin with plastic wrap and refrigerate for at least 2 hours, or overnight, until well chilled and set.
9. **Caramelize the Sugar:**
    - Just before serving, sprinkle a thin, even layer of granulated sugar over each custard. Use a kitchen torch to caramelize the sugar until it melts and forms a golden-brown crust. Alternatively, you can place the ramekins under a broiler set to high for 1-2 minutes, watching closely to avoid burning.
10. **Serve:**
    - Let the Crème Brûlée sit for a minute to allow the caramelized sugar to harden. Garnish with fresh berries or mint leaves if desired, and serve immediately.

Tips:

- **Vanilla:** Using a vanilla bean gives a richer flavor, but you can substitute with pure vanilla extract if needed.
- **Water Bath:** Ensuring the water bath is gently simmering helps cook the custards evenly without curdling.
- **Caramelizing Sugar:** Aim for a thin, even layer of sugar for the best caramelization. Hold the torch about 2-3 inches away from the surface for even melting.

Enjoy the luxurious and creamy texture of Crème Brûlée, contrasted with the satisfying crack of caramelized sugar on top, for a delightful ending to any meal.

Pâté en Croûte (Pâté in Pastry)

Ingredients:

For the Pâté Filling:

- 1 lb (450g) pork shoulder, coarsely ground
- 8 oz (225g) chicken livers, trimmed and chopped
- 8 oz (225g) pork belly, coarsely ground
- 1 small onion, finely chopped
- 2 cloves garlic, minced
- 1/4 cup brandy or cognac
- 1/4 cup heavy cream
- 2 tablespoons chopped fresh parsley
- 1 tablespoon chopped fresh thyme leaves
- 1 teaspoon ground allspice
- 1 teaspoon ground cloves
- 1 teaspoon ground nutmeg
- Salt and freshly ground black pepper, to taste

For the Pastry:

- 1 lb (450g) puff pastry, store-bought or homemade
- 1 egg, beaten (for egg wash)

Instructions:

1. **Prepare the Pâté Filling:**
    - In a large mixing bowl, combine the coarsely ground pork shoulder, chicken livers, and pork belly.
    - Add chopped onion, minced garlic, brandy or cognac, heavy cream, chopped parsley, thyme leaves, allspice, cloves, nutmeg, salt, and pepper.
    - Mix everything together thoroughly until well combined. Cover and refrigerate for at least 2 hours or overnight to allow the flavors to meld.
2. **Prepare the Pastry and Assembly:**
    - Preheat your oven to 375°F (190°C). Line a baking sheet with parchment paper.
    - Roll out the puff pastry on a lightly floured surface into a rectangle large enough to encase the pâté filling.
    - Place half of the pâté filling lengthwise down the center of the pastry rectangle, leaving about 1 inch of pastry on each side.
3. **Shape and Seal the Pâté:**
    - Fold the sides of the pastry over the pâté filling, overlapping slightly in the center. Press the edges to seal.
    - Place the remaining half of the pâté filling on top of the pastry-covered pâté.

- Fold the pastry over the top, sealing the edges to encase the pâté completely. Trim any excess pastry if necessary.
4. **Decorate and Bake:**
   - Use a sharp knife to score decorative patterns or vents on the top of the pastry.
   - Brush the entire surface of the pastry with beaten egg wash.
5. **Bake the Pâté:**
   - Place the assembled Pâté en Croûte on the prepared baking sheet.
   - Bake in the preheated oven for 50-60 minutes, or until the pastry is golden brown and cooked through. The internal temperature of the pâté should reach 160°F (71°C).
6. **Cool and Serve:**
   - Remove the Pâté en Croûte from the oven and let it cool on a wire rack for at least 20 minutes before slicing.
   - Serve warm or at room temperature, sliced into portions.

Tips:

- **Meat Mixture:** The mixture of pork shoulder, chicken livers, and pork belly gives the pâté its rich and flavorful texture. Ensure the meats are well combined and seasoned.
- **Puff Pastry:** Puff pastry should be rolled out evenly to ensure even baking and a crisp texture. If using store-bought pastry, follow package instructions for thawing and handling.
- **Resting Time:** Allowing the pâté filling to rest in the refrigerator helps the flavors to develop and meld together.

Pâté en Croûte is a wonderful dish for special occasions or as an impressive appetizer for a gathering. Enjoy the combination of savory pâté and buttery pastry, traditionally served with pickles, mustard, or a simple salad.

Soupe à l'Oignon (French Onion Soup)

Ingredients:

- 4 large onions, thinly sliced
- 3 tablespoons unsalted butter
- 1 tablespoon olive oil
- 2 cloves garlic, minced
- 1/2 cup dry white wine (optional)
- 6 cups beef broth (homemade or low-sodium store-bought)
- 1 bay leaf
- 1 teaspoon chopped fresh thyme (or 1/2 teaspoon dried thyme)
- Salt and freshly ground black pepper, to taste
- 4-6 slices of baguette or French bread, toasted
- 1 1/2 cups grated Gruyère cheese (or Swiss cheese)
- Chopped fresh parsley, for garnish

Instructions:

1. **Caramelize the Onions:**
   - In a large pot or Dutch oven, melt the butter and olive oil over medium heat.
   - Add the thinly sliced onions and cook slowly, stirring occasionally, until the onions are deeply golden brown and caramelized, about 30-40 minutes. Be patient during this step as it's crucial for developing rich flavor.
2. **Deglaze the Pan:**
   - Add minced garlic to the caramelized onions and cook for another 1-2 minutes until fragrant.
   - If using, pour in the white wine to deglaze the pan, scraping up any browned bits from the bottom. Let it simmer for a few minutes until the wine has reduced slightly.
3. **Simmer the Soup:**
   - Pour in the beef broth and add the bay leaf and chopped thyme.
   - Season with salt and pepper to taste. Bring the soup to a simmer and cook for 20-30 minutes to allow the flavors to meld together. Taste and adjust seasoning if needed.
4. **Prepare the Bread and Cheese:**
   - Preheat your oven's broiler.
   - Ladle the hot soup into oven-safe bowls or crocks. Top each bowl with a slice of toasted baguette.
   - Sprinkle a generous amount of grated Gruyère cheese (or Swiss cheese) over the bread and soup.
5. **Broil the Soup:**
   - Place the bowls on a baking sheet and transfer them under the broiler. Broil for 2-3 minutes, or until the cheese is melted, bubbly, and golden brown.

- Keep a close eye on the soup to prevent burning.
6. **Serve:**
    - Carefully remove the bowls from the oven (they will be hot!). Garnish with chopped fresh parsley for added freshness and color.
    - Serve immediately while hot and enjoy the delicious, comforting French Onion Soup.

Tips:

- **Onions:** Use a combination of yellow and red onions for a balanced flavor profile. Slice them thinly and cook them slowly to achieve caramelization.
- **Cheese:** Gruyère cheese is traditional for French Onion Soup due to its nutty flavor and melting properties. However, you can also use Swiss cheese or a combination of both.
- **Bread:** Choose a crusty baguette or French bread, slice it, and toast it until golden and crisp before adding it to the soup.

French Onion Soup is perfect for cold winter days or whenever you crave a hearty and warming soup with layers of savory flavors. It's a favorite among many for its rich broth, sweet caramelized onions, and gooey cheese topping.

Steak Frites

Ingredients:

- 2 beef steaks (such as ribeye, sirloin, or filet mignon), about 8-10 ounces each
- Salt and freshly ground black pepper
- 2 tablespoons olive oil or vegetable oil
- 4 tablespoons unsalted butter
- 4 cloves garlic, minced (optional)
- Fresh herbs (such as thyme or rosemary), chopped (optional)
- Fresh parsley, chopped (for garnish)

For the French Fries:

- 4 large potatoes (Russet or Yukon Gold), peeled and cut into sticks
- Vegetable oil, for frying
- Salt, to taste

Instructions:

For the French Fries:

1. **Prepare the Potatoes:**
   - Peel the potatoes and cut them into sticks, about 1/4-inch thick. Rinse the potato sticks under cold water to remove excess starch.
2. **Preheat the Oil:**
   - Heat vegetable oil in a deep fryer or large pot to 325°F (160°C). Alternatively, you can use a deep, heavy-bottomed skillet.
3. **Blanch the Fries:**
   - Working in batches, carefully add the potato sticks to the hot oil. Fry for about 4-5 minutes per batch, until they are just starting to become tender but not yet golden. Remove with a slotted spoon and drain on paper towels. Let them cool completely.
4. **Final Fry:**
   - Increase the oil temperature to 375°F (190°C).
   - Return the blanched fries to the hot oil in batches, frying until they are golden brown and crispy, about 2-3 minutes per batch. Remove with a slotted spoon and drain on paper towels. Season with salt while still hot.

For the Steak:

1. **Prepare the Steaks:**
   - Pat the steaks dry with paper towels. Season generously with salt and pepper on both sides.
2. **Cook the Steaks:**

- Heat 2 tablespoons of olive oil (or vegetable oil) in a large skillet over medium-high heat until hot but not smoking.
- Add the steaks to the skillet and cook to your desired doneness, flipping once. Cooking times will vary depending on the thickness of the steaks and your preferred doneness (about 3-4 minutes per side for medium-rare, for example).
- Optional: In the last minute of cooking, add 2 tablespoons of butter to the skillet along with minced garlic and fresh herbs (if using). Baste the steaks with the melted butter and herbs.

3. **Rest the Steaks:**
    - Remove the steaks from the skillet and let them rest on a cutting board or plate for a few minutes.
4. **Serve:**
    - Slice the steaks against the grain into thick slices.
    - Arrange the steak slices on plates alongside a generous serving of crispy French fries.
    - Garnish with chopped fresh parsley and serve immediately.

Tips:

- **Steak Doneness:** Use a meat thermometer to check the internal temperature of the steaks for accuracy: 120-125°F (49-52°C) for rare, 130-135°F (54-57°C) for medium-rare, 140-145°F (60-63°C) for medium, and 150-155°F (66-68°C) for medium-well.
- **French Fries:** Double-frying the fries ensures they are crispy on the outside and fluffy on the inside. Make sure to drain them well on paper towels after each frying session.
- **Variations:** Feel free to customize by adding your favorite steak seasoning or sauces like Béarnaise sauce or peppercorn sauce.

Enjoy this classic French bistro favorite of Steak Frites with its perfect combination of tender steak and crispy fries, all seasoned and cooked to perfection!

Profiteroles

Ingredients:

For the Choux Pastry:

- 1/2 cup (1 stick) unsalted butter
- 1 cup water
- 1/4 teaspoon salt
- 1 cup all-purpose flour
- 4 large eggs

For the Filling:

- 1 1/2 cups heavy cream
- 2 tablespoons powdered sugar
- 1 teaspoon vanilla extract

For the Chocolate Sauce:

- 4 ounces semisweet or bittersweet chocolate, chopped
- 1/2 cup heavy cream
- 1 tablespoon unsalted butter
- 1 tablespoon corn syrup (optional, for shine)

Instructions:

For the Choux Pastry:

1. **Preheat Oven:**
   - Preheat your oven to 400°F (200°C). Line a baking sheet with parchment paper or a silicone baking mat.
2. **Prepare the Choux Pastry:**
   - In a medium saucepan, combine the butter, water, and salt. Bring to a boil over medium heat.
   - Add the flour all at once and stir vigorously with a wooden spoon until the mixture forms a ball and pulls away from the sides of the pan. This is the choux pastry dough.
3. **Cool the Dough:**
   - Transfer the dough to a mixing bowl and let it cool slightly, about 5 minutes.
4. **Add Eggs:**
   - Add the eggs one at a time, beating well after each addition, until the dough is smooth and glossy. It should be thick enough to pipe but still able to slowly fall from a spoon.
5. **Pipe the Dough:**

- Transfer the choux pastry dough to a pastry bag fitted with a large round tip (or use a zip-top bag with a corner cut off). Pipe small mounds onto the prepared baking sheet, about 1 1/2 inches in diameter and 1 inch apart.

6. **Bake:**
   - Bake in the preheated oven for 15 minutes, then reduce the oven temperature to 350°F (175°C) and bake for an additional 20-25 minutes, or until the profiteroles are golden brown and puffed. Do not open the oven door during baking to prevent them from deflating.
   - Remove from the oven and transfer to a wire rack to cool completely.

For the Filling:

1. **Whip the Cream:**
   - In a chilled mixing bowl, whip the heavy cream, powdered sugar, and vanilla extract until stiff peaks form.
2. **Fill the Profiteroles:**
   - Once the profiteroles are completely cooled, use a small knife or pastry tip to make a small hole in the bottom of each profiterole.
   - Pipe or spoon the whipped cream filling into each profiterole until filled.

For the Chocolate Sauce:

1. **Make the Chocolate Sauce:**
   - In a small saucepan, heat the heavy cream until it just begins to simmer.
   - Remove from heat and add the chopped chocolate, butter, and corn syrup (if using). Let it sit for a minute, then stir until smooth and glossy.

Assembly:

1. **Serve:**
   - Arrange the filled profiteroles on a serving platter or individual plates.
   - Drizzle the warm chocolate sauce over the profiteroles.
2. **Optional Garnish:**
   - Dust with powdered sugar or top with additional whipped cream if desired.

Tips:

- **Choux Pastry:** The key to successful choux pastry is to cook the flour and butter mixture until it forms a smooth ball and then incorporate the eggs one at a time until the dough is smooth and glossy.
- **Filling:** The whipped cream filling can be flavored with other extracts like almond or coffee for variation.
- **Chocolate Sauce:** For a shiny finish, add corn syrup to the chocolate sauce.

Enjoy these homemade profiteroles as a delightful dessert, perfect for any occasion with their light and airy pastry filled with creamy goodness and topped with decadent chocolate sauce!

Coquilles Saint-Jacques (Scallops in Cream Sauce)

Ingredients:

- 1 lb (450g) fresh scallops, cleaned and patted dry
- Salt and freshly ground black pepper, to taste
- 2 tablespoons unsalted butter
- 1 shallot, finely chopped
- 2 cloves garlic, minced
- 1/2 cup dry white wine
- 1 cup heavy cream
- 1/2 cup grated Gruyère cheese (optional, for topping)
- Fresh parsley, chopped, for garnish
- Lemon wedges, for serving

For the Breadcrumbs (optional topping):

- 1/2 cup breadcrumbs
- 2 tablespoons unsalted butter, melted
- 1 tablespoon chopped fresh parsley

Instructions:

1. **Prepare the Scallops:**
    - Preheat your oven to 400°F (200°C).
    - Season the scallops with salt and pepper on both sides.
2. **Sear the Scallops:**
    - In a large skillet, melt 1 tablespoon of butter over medium-high heat.
    - Add the scallops in a single layer (work in batches if necessary to avoid overcrowding) and sear for 1-2 minutes per side until golden brown. Transfer the seared scallops to a plate and set aside.
3. **Make the Sauce:**
    - In the same skillet, add the remaining 1 tablespoon of butter.
    - Add the chopped shallot and minced garlic. Cook for 2-3 minutes until softened and fragrant.
    - Pour in the white wine and cook for another 2-3 minutes, allowing the wine to reduce by half.
4. **Add the Cream:**
    - Lower the heat to medium-low and pour in the heavy cream. Stir well to combine.
    - Simmer gently for 5-7 minutes, stirring occasionally, until the sauce thickens slightly.
5. **Assemble and Bake:**
    - Arrange the seared scallops in individual gratin dishes or a shallow baking dish.
    - Pour the cream sauce evenly over the scallops.

6. **Optional Topping:**
   - In a small bowl, combine the breadcrumbs, melted butter, and chopped parsley.
   - Sprinkle the breadcrumb mixture evenly over the scallops and sauce.
   - If using, sprinkle grated Gruyère cheese on top for an extra layer of flavor.
7. **Bake:**
   - Place the gratin dishes or baking dish in the preheated oven.
   - Bake for 10-12 minutes, or until the scallops are cooked through and the sauce is bubbly and lightly golden on top.
8. **Serve:**
   - Remove from the oven and let it cool for a few minutes.
   - Garnish with chopped parsley and serve hot, accompanied by lemon wedges on the side.

Tips:

- **Scallops:** Use fresh scallops and ensure they are dried well with paper towels before cooking to achieve a nice sear.
- **Sauce:** The cream sauce should be simmered gently to allow it to thicken slightly and infuse with flavors from the shallots, garlic, and white wine.
- **Variations:** Feel free to customize by adding mushrooms, spinach, or a touch of Dijon mustard to the sauce for extra depth of flavor.

Coquilles Saint-Jacques makes for an elegant and indulgent main course, perfect for a special dinner at home. Serve it with crusty bread or over rice to soak up the delicious creamy sauce.

Mousse au Chocolat

Ingredients:

- 7 ounces (200g) dark chocolate (at least 70% cocoa), chopped
- 4 large eggs, separated
- 1/4 cup (50g) granulated sugar
- 1/2 teaspoon vanilla extract
- Pinch of salt
- Whipped cream, for serving (optional)
- Chocolate shavings or cocoa powder, for garnish (optional)

Instructions:

1. **Melt the Chocolate:**
   - Place the chopped dark chocolate in a heatproof bowl. You can either melt it in the microwave in short bursts, stirring frequently, or melt it over a double boiler until smooth. Set aside to cool slightly.
2. **Prepare the Egg Yolks:**
   - In a large mixing bowl, whisk the egg yolks with half of the granulated sugar until pale and creamy.
3. **Combine with Chocolate:**
   - Gradually pour the melted chocolate into the egg yolk mixture, whisking constantly until well combined. Stir in the vanilla extract.
4. **Whip the Egg Whites:**
   - In a separate clean bowl, using a hand mixer or a stand mixer fitted with the whisk attachment, beat the egg whites with a pinch of salt until soft peaks form.
   - Gradually add the remaining granulated sugar and continue beating until stiff peaks form.
5. **Incorporate Egg Whites:**
   - Gently fold a spoonful of the beaten egg whites into the chocolate mixture to lighten it. Then, carefully fold in the remaining egg whites in two or three additions, using a spatula. Be gentle to maintain the mousse's light and airy texture.
6. **Chill the Mousse:**
   - Spoon the chocolate mousse into serving glasses or bowls. Cover and refrigerate for at least 2-3 hours, or until set.
7. **Serve:**
   - Before serving, garnish with a dollop of whipped cream, chocolate shavings, or a dusting of cocoa powder, if desired.

Tips:

- **Chocolate:** Use good quality dark chocolate with at least 70% cocoa for a rich and intense flavor. You can also use semi-sweet or bittersweet chocolate according to your preference.
- **Eggs:** Make sure to separate the eggs carefully and avoid getting any yolk into the whites, as this can prevent the egg whites from whipping properly.
- **Folding Technique:** When folding the beaten egg whites into the chocolate mixture, use a gentle motion to combine them thoroughly while keeping the mousse light and fluffy.

Enjoy this classic Mousse au Chocolat as a decadent and elegant dessert, perfect for any occasion, from a casual dinner to a special celebration. The silky smooth texture and deep chocolate flavor are sure to impress!

Poulet à la Provençale (Provençal Chicken)

Ingredients:

- 4 bone-in, skin-on chicken thighs
- Salt and freshly ground black pepper, to taste
- 2 tablespoons olive oil
- 1 onion, finely chopped
- 3 cloves garlic, minced
- 1 red bell pepper, sliced
- 1 yellow bell pepper, sliced
- 1 can (14 oz) diced tomatoes, with juices
- 1/2 cup pitted black olives (such as Kalamata), halved
- 1 teaspoon herbes de Provence (or a mix of dried thyme, rosemary, oregano)
- 1/2 cup chicken broth or white wine
- Fresh basil or parsley, chopped, for garnish

Instructions:

1. **Season and Sear the Chicken:**
    - Season the chicken thighs generously with salt and pepper on both sides.
    - In a large skillet or Dutch oven, heat the olive oil over medium-high heat. Add the chicken thighs, skin-side down, and sear until golden brown, about 4-5 minutes per side. Remove the chicken from the skillet and set aside.
2. **Sauté Vegetables:**
    - In the same skillet, add the chopped onion and sauté for 3-4 minutes until softened.
    - Add the minced garlic and sliced bell peppers. Cook for another 2-3 minutes until the peppers start to soften.
3. **Combine Ingredients:**
    - Stir in the diced tomatoes with their juices, black olives, and herbes de Provence. Cook for 1-2 minutes to combine the flavors.
4. **Add Chicken and Liquid:**
    - Return the seared chicken thighs back to the skillet, nestling them into the vegetable mixture.
    - Pour in the chicken broth or white wine around the chicken thighs.
5. **Simmer:**
    - Bring the mixture to a simmer. Reduce the heat to medium-low, cover the skillet, and let it simmer gently for 25-30 minutes, or until the chicken is cooked through and tender. Stir occasionally and check for seasoning.
6. **Serve:**
    - Remove from heat and garnish with chopped fresh basil or parsley.
    - Serve Poulet à la Provençale hot, spooning the flavorful tomato and olive mixture over the chicken.

Tips:

- **Chicken Thighs:** Bone-in, skin-on chicken thighs are ideal for this dish as they stay moist and flavorful during cooking. You can also use chicken drumsticks or a combination of thighs and drumsticks.
- **Herbes de Provence:** This traditional blend typically includes dried thyme, rosemary, oregano, marjoram, and sometimes lavender flowers. It adds an aromatic and earthy flavor to the dish, but you can adjust the herbs according to your taste.
- **Vegetables:** Feel free to customize with other vegetables such as zucchini, eggplant, or mushrooms, depending on what's in season or your preferences.

Poulet à la Provençale is perfect served with crusty bread or over rice, couscous, or mashed potatoes to soak up the delicious sauce. It's a hearty and satisfying dish that captures the essence of Provencal cuisine with its vibrant colors and robust flavors.

Galette des Rois (King Cake)

Ingredients:

For the Pastry:

- 2 sheets of store-bought puff pastry (about 9-10 inches/23-25 cm each), thawed if frozen
- 1 egg yolk mixed with 1 tablespoon milk (for egg wash)
- Powdered sugar, for dusting

For the Almond Filling (Frangipane):

- 1/2 cup (115g) unsalted butter, softened
- 1/2 cup (100g) granulated sugar
- 1 cup (100g) ground almonds (almond meal)
- 2 large eggs
- 1 teaspoon almond extract
- 1 tablespoon all-purpose flour
- 1 dry bean or figurine (optional, for hiding inside the galette)

Instructions:

1. **Prepare the Almond Filling (Frangipane):**
    - In a mixing bowl, cream together the softened butter and granulated sugar until pale and fluffy.
    - Add the ground almonds, eggs, almond extract, and flour. Mix until well combined. Set aside.
2. **Assemble the Galette:**
    - Preheat your oven to 400°F (200°C). Line a baking sheet with parchment paper.
    - Place one sheet of puff pastry on the prepared baking sheet.
    - Spoon the almond filling (frangipane) onto the center of the pastry sheet, leaving about 1 inch (2.5 cm) border around the edges.
    - Optional: Place a dry bean or figurine somewhere in the filling (traditionally to symbolize finding the king or queen).
3. **Cover with Second Pastry Sheet:**
    - Brush the edges of the bottom pastry sheet with water to help seal.
    - Place the second sheet of puff pastry on top and press down gently around the edges to seal.
    - Trim any excess pastry if necessary, and crimp the edges with a fork to seal further.
4. **Decorate:**
    - Using a sharp knife, lightly score the top of the galette in a decorative pattern (such as crisscross or spiral).
    - Brush the top of the galette with the egg wash (egg yolk mixed with milk).
5. **Bake:**

- Bake in the preheated oven for 25-30 minutes, or until the galette is golden brown and puffed up.
    - Remove from the oven and let it cool slightly on a wire rack.
6. **Serve:**
    - Dust the galette with powdered sugar before serving.
    - Traditionally, the galette is cut into slices and served warm or at room temperature.

Serving Tradition:

- In France, it's customary to serve Galette des Rois during the Epiphany season. The person who finds the hidden bean or figurine in their slice is crowned king or queen for the day and may wear a paper crown (included with many store-bought galettes).

Tips:

- **Puff Pastry:** If using frozen puff pastry, thaw it according to package instructions before assembling the galette.
- **Almond Filling:** Ensure the butter is softened for easier mixing with other ingredients to form a smooth frangipane.
- **Decoration:** Feel free to get creative with your galette's decoration, but remember to score lightly to avoid cutting through the pastry completely.

Enjoy this delicious Galette des Rois with family and friends as a delightful treat that celebrates tradition and indulgence during the festive season!

Gratin Dauphinois

Ingredients:

- 2 lbs (about 1 kg) potatoes (preferably Russet or Yukon Gold), peeled and thinly sliced (about 1/8 inch thick)
- 2 cups (480 ml) heavy cream
- 1 cup (240 ml) whole milk
- 2 cloves garlic, minced or thinly sliced
- Salt and freshly ground black pepper, to taste
- Pinch of nutmeg (optional)
- 1 cup (100 g) shredded Gruyère cheese (optional, for topping)
- Butter, for greasing the baking dish

Instructions:

1. **Preheat Oven:**
   - Preheat your oven to 375°F (190°C). Butter a 9x13 inch (23x33 cm) baking dish or a gratin dish.
2. **Prepare Potatoes:**
   - Peel the potatoes and slice them thinly, about 1/8 inch thick. A mandoline slicer can be helpful for achieving even slices.
3. **Make the Cream Mixture:**
   - In a medium saucepan, combine the heavy cream, milk, minced garlic, salt, pepper, and nutmeg (if using). Heat over medium heat until it just begins to simmer. Remove from heat.
4. **Layer Potatoes in Dish:**
   - Arrange a layer of sliced potatoes evenly in the buttered baking dish, slightly overlapping each slice.
5. **Pour Cream Mixture:**
   - Pour a portion of the hot cream mixture over the potatoes, enough to cover them.
   - Repeat layering potatoes and pouring cream mixture until all potatoes and cream are used, finishing with a layer of potatoes on top.
6. **Bake:**
   - Cover the baking dish with aluminum foil and place it in the preheated oven.
   - Bake for 45 minutes to 1 hour, or until the potatoes are tender when pierced with a fork.
7. **Add Cheese (Optional):**
   - If using cheese, uncover the dish and sprinkle shredded Gruyère cheese over the top of the gratin during the last 10-15 minutes of baking. This will allow the cheese to melt and become golden and bubbly.
8. **Serve:**
   - Once cooked, remove the gratin from the oven and let it rest for a few minutes before serving. This allows the cream to thicken slightly.

- Serve Gratin Dauphinois hot, garnished with fresh chopped parsley if desired.

Tips:

- **Potatoes:** Choose starchy potatoes like Russet or Yukon Gold for the best texture in this dish. Slice them thinly and evenly for even cooking.
- **Cream Mixture:** Heating the cream mixture before pouring it over the potatoes ensures even cooking and absorption of flavors.
- **Cheese:** Gruyère cheese adds a delicious nutty flavor, but you can also use other cheeses like Emmental or Parmesan.

Gratin Dauphinois is a comforting and indulgent side dish that pairs well with roasted meats, poultry, or as part of a festive holiday meal. Enjoy its creamy, savory goodness straight from the oven!

Navarin d'Agneau (Lamb Stew)

Ingredients:

- 2 lbs (about 1 kg) lamb shoulder or leg, cut into cubes
- Salt and freshly ground black pepper, to taste
- 2 tablespoons all-purpose flour
- 2 tablespoons olive oil
- 1 onion, diced
- 2 cloves garlic, minced
- 2 carrots, peeled and cut into chunks
- 2 celery stalks, sliced
- 1 cup (240 ml) dry white wine
- 4 cups (1 liter) chicken or lamb broth
- 2 bay leaves
- 1 teaspoon dried thyme (or 2-3 sprigs fresh thyme)
- 1 lb (about 500 g) baby potatoes, halved or quartered
- 1 cup (150 g) fresh or frozen peas
- Chopped fresh parsley, for garnish

Instructions:

1. **Prepare the Lamb:**
    - Pat the lamb cubes dry with paper towels. Season generously with salt and pepper.
    - Dredge the lamb pieces in flour, shaking off any excess.
2. **Brown the Lamb:**
    - In a large Dutch oven or heavy-bottomed pot, heat the olive oil over medium-high heat.
    - Add the lamb cubes in batches, ensuring not to overcrowd the pot. Brown the lamb on all sides until golden brown. Remove the lamb from the pot and set aside.
3. **Sauté the Vegetables:**
    - In the same pot, add the diced onion and sauté for 3-4 minutes until softened.
    - Add the minced garlic, carrots, and celery. Cook for another 3-4 minutes until the vegetables begin to soften.
4. **Deglaze and Simmer:**
    - Pour in the white wine, scraping up any browned bits from the bottom of the pot with a wooden spoon.
    - Return the browned lamb to the pot.
    - Add the chicken or lamb broth, bay leaves, and dried thyme (if using fresh thyme, tie the sprigs together with kitchen twine for easy removal later).
    - Bring the mixture to a boil, then reduce the heat to low. Cover the pot and let it simmer gently for 1.5 to 2 hours, or until the lamb is tender and cooked through.

5. **Add Potatoes and Peas:**
    - Add the halved or quartered baby potatoes to the pot. Simmer, uncovered, for another 20-25 minutes until the potatoes are fork-tender.
6. **Finish and Serve:**
    - Stir in the fresh or frozen peas and cook for an additional 5 minutes until the peas are heated through.
    - Remove the bay leaves and thyme sprigs (if using).
    - Taste and adjust seasoning with salt and pepper if needed.
    - Garnish with chopped fresh parsley before serving.

Serving Suggestions:

- Navarin d'Agneau is traditionally served hot, garnished with fresh parsley, alongside crusty bread or over steamed rice.
- It pairs well with a glass of red wine, such as a Bordeaux or Côtes du Rhône, to complement the rich flavors of the stew.

Tips:

- **Lamb:** Use boneless lamb shoulder or leg for this stew. Trim excess fat and cut into evenly sized cubes for even cooking.
- **Vegetables:** Feel free to add other seasonal vegetables such as pearl onions, turnips, or green beans to customize the stew.
- **Broth:** Opt for homemade broth for the best flavor, or use a good-quality store-bought broth.

Enjoy this comforting and hearty Navarin d'Agneau, perfect for a cozy family dinner or a special occasion meal.

Îles Flottantes (Floating Islands)

Ingredients:

For the Meringue:

- 4 large eggs, separated
- 1/2 cup (100 g) granulated sugar
- 1/2 teaspoon vanilla extract
- Pinch of salt

For the Custard (Crème Anglaise):

- 2 cups (480 ml) whole milk
- 1 vanilla bean, split lengthwise (or 1 teaspoon vanilla extract)
- 4 large egg yolks
- 1/2 cup (100 g) granulated sugar

For Garnish:

- Caramel sauce or praline (optional)
- Toasted sliced almonds or crushed pistachios (optional)

Instructions:

1. Make the Custard (Crème Anglaise):

1. In a saucepan, heat the milk over medium heat until it just begins to simmer. Add the split vanilla bean (if using) and let it steep for 10-15 minutes to infuse the milk with vanilla flavor. Remove the vanilla bean pod.
2. In a bowl, whisk together the egg yolks and sugar until pale and creamy.
3. Gradually pour the hot milk into the egg yolk mixture, whisking constantly to prevent the eggs from curdling.
4. Return the mixture to the saucepan and cook over low heat, stirring constantly with a wooden spoon or spatula, until the custard thickens enough to coat the back of the spoon. This should take about 5-8 minutes. Do not let it boil.
5. Once thickened, remove from heat and strain the custard through a fine-mesh sieve into a bowl to remove any cooked egg bits. Stir in the vanilla extract (if using instead of vanilla bean). Cover with plastic wrap directly on the surface of the custard to prevent a skin from forming. Chill in the refrigerator until ready to use.

2. Make the Meringue:

1. In a clean, dry mixing bowl, beat the egg whites with a pinch of salt using an electric mixer on medium speed until soft peaks form.

2. Gradually add the granulated sugar, a spoonful at a time, while continuing to beat on high speed until the meringue is glossy and stiff peaks form.
3. Gently fold in the vanilla extract using a spatula.

3. Poach the Meringue:

1. Bring a large pot of water to a simmer. Shape the meringue into oval-shaped quenelles (or simply use two large spoons) and gently poach them in the simmering water for about 3-4 minutes per side, or until they are firm and cooked through. You may need to do this in batches depending on the size of your pot.
2. Remove the poached meringues with a slotted spoon and place them on a plate lined with paper towels to drain excess water.

4. Assemble the Îles Flottantes:

1. Divide the chilled custard (crème anglaise) among serving bowls or plates.
2. Place one or two poached meringues on top of each serving of custard.
3. Drizzle with caramel sauce or sprinkle with praline (if using).
4. Optionally, garnish with toasted sliced almonds or crushed pistachios.

5. Serve:

- Serve Îles Flottantes immediately or chill briefly in the refrigerator before serving. Enjoy this elegant and light French dessert!

Tips:

- **Meringue Poaching:** Ensure the water is at a gentle simmer, not boiling, to prevent the meringue from falling apart.
- **Custard Consistency:** The custard should be thick enough to coat the back of a spoon but not too thick. If it becomes too thick, whisk in a little more milk to adjust the consistency.
- **Flavor Variations:** Experiment with different toppings such as fresh berries or a drizzle of chocolate sauce for a twist on this classic dessert.

Îles Flottantes is a delightful dessert that combines the airy texture of meringue with the creamy richness of custard, making it a perfect ending to any meal.

Lapin à la Moutarde (Mustard Rabbit)

Ingredients:

- 1 whole rabbit, about 2.5-3 lbs (1.1-1.4 kg), cut into serving pieces
- Salt and freshly ground black pepper, to taste
- 2 tablespoons olive oil
- 4 tablespoons unsalted butter
- 1 onion, finely chopped
- 2 cloves garlic, minced
- 1/2 cup dry white wine
- 1 cup chicken broth
- 3 tablespoons Dijon mustard
- 2 tablespoons whole grain mustard
- 1/2 cup heavy cream (optional, for a richer sauce)
- 2 tablespoons chopped fresh parsley, for garnish

Instructions:

1. **Prepare the Rabbit:**
   - Rinse the rabbit pieces under cold water and pat dry with paper towels. Season generously with salt and pepper.
2. **Brown the Rabbit:**
   - In a large Dutch oven or heavy-bottomed pot, heat the olive oil and 2 tablespoons of butter over medium-high heat.
   - Add the rabbit pieces in batches, making sure not to overcrowd the pot. Brown the rabbit on all sides until golden brown. Remove the rabbit pieces from the pot and set aside.
3. **Sauté Onion and Garlic:**
   - In the same pot, add the chopped onion and sauté for 3-4 minutes until softened.
   - Add the minced garlic and cook for another minute until fragrant.
4. **Deglaze with Wine:**
   - Pour in the white wine and bring to a boil, scraping up any browned bits from the bottom of the pot with a wooden spoon.
5. **Simmer with Broth and Mustard:**
   - Return the rabbit pieces to the pot.
   - Add the chicken broth, Dijon mustard, and whole grain mustard. Stir to combine.
6. **Braise the Rabbit:**
   - Reduce the heat to low, cover the pot, and let the rabbit simmer gently for about 1 hour, or until the rabbit is tender and cooked through. Stir occasionally.
7. **Finish the Sauce:**
   - Stir in the heavy cream (if using) and simmer for another 5-10 minutes until the sauce thickens slightly.
8. **Serve:**

- Remove from heat and stir in the remaining 2 tablespoons of butter until melted and incorporated into the sauce.
- Taste and adjust seasoning with salt and pepper if needed.
- Sprinkle with chopped fresh parsley before serving.

Serving Suggestions:

- Lapin à la Moutarde is traditionally served hot, accompanied by crusty bread or over steamed rice to soak up the delicious mustard sauce.
- Pair with a glass of white wine, such as a Chardonnay or Sauvignon Blanc, to complement the flavors of the dish.

Tips:

- **Rabbit Preparation:** If you're not familiar with preparing rabbit, ask your butcher to cut it into pieces for you.
- **Mustard:** The combination of Dijon mustard and whole grain mustard adds depth and flavor to the sauce. Adjust the amount to your taste preferences.
- **Cream (optional):** Adding heavy cream enriches the sauce and gives it a velvety texture, but you can omit it for a lighter dish.

Enjoy this hearty and flavorful Lapin à la Moutarde, a quintessential French dish that highlights the delicate taste of rabbit with the bold flavors of mustard!

Gougères (Cheese Puffs)

Ingredients:

- 1 cup water
- 6 tablespoons unsalted butter, cut into pieces
- 1/2 teaspoon salt
- 1 cup all-purpose flour
- 4 large eggs
- 1 1/2 cups grated Gruyère cheese (or similar cheese like Comté or Emmental)
- Freshly ground black pepper, to taste
- Pinch of nutmeg (optional)
- Egg wash (1 egg beaten with 1 tablespoon water), for brushing

Instructions:

1. **Preheat Oven:**
    - Preheat your oven to 400°F (200°C). Line a baking sheet with parchment paper.
2. **Prepare Choux Pastry:**
    - In a medium saucepan, combine water, butter, and salt. Bring to a boil over medium-high heat.
3. **Add Flour:**
    - Reduce heat to low and add flour all at once. Stir vigorously with a wooden spoon until the mixture forms a ball and pulls away from the sides of the pan. This should take about 1 minute.
4. **Cool Mixture:**
    - Remove from heat and let cool for a couple of minutes.
5. **Add Eggs:**
    - Add eggs one at a time, beating well after each addition, until the mixture is smooth and glossy. It may initially appear lumpy but will smooth out as you continue to mix.
6. **Add Cheese and Seasoning:**
    - Stir in grated Gruyère cheese, black pepper, and nutmeg (if using), mixing until well combined.
7. **Form and Bake:**
    - Using a spoon or a piping bag fitted with a large round tip, drop tablespoons of dough onto the prepared baking sheet, spacing them about 2 inches (5 cm) apart.
8. **Brush with Egg Wash:**
    - Brush the tops of each gougère with egg wash.
9. **Bake:**
    - Bake in the preheated oven for 15-20 minutes, or until puffed and golden brown.
10. **Cool and Serve:**
    - Remove from the oven and let cool on a wire rack for a few minutes.

- Serve warm or at room temperature.

Serving Suggestions:

- Gougères are best served fresh and warm, straight from the oven.
- They can be enjoyed on their own as appetizers or alongside salads, soups, or as part of a cheese board.

Tips:

- **Cheese:** Gruyère is traditional, but you can experiment with other cheeses like Comté, Emmental, or even a sharp cheddar.
- **Consistency:** The dough should be thick enough to hold its shape when dropped onto the baking sheet but still light and airy when baked.
- **Variations:** Add herbs like thyme or rosemary for extra flavor, or substitute black pepper with cayenne pepper for a bit of heat.

Enjoy these homemade Gougères as a delightful addition to any gathering or as a special treat for yourself!

Pain Perdu (French Toast)

Ingredients:

- 4 slices of thick-cut bread (French bread or brioche works well)
- 2 large eggs
- 1/2 cup milk
- 1/4 teaspoon vanilla extract
- 1 tablespoon granulated sugar (optional)
- Pinch of salt
- Butter or neutral oil for cooking
- Powdered sugar, maple syrup, fresh berries, or other toppings (optional)

Instructions:

1. **Prepare the Bread:**
   - If your bread is very fresh, you can lightly toast it to prevent it from becoming too soggy when soaked in the egg mixture.
2. **Prepare the Egg Mixture:**
   - In a shallow bowl or pie plate, whisk together the eggs, milk, vanilla extract, sugar (if using), and a pinch of salt until well combined.
3. **Soak the Bread:**
   - Heat a large skillet or griddle over medium heat and add a knob of butter or a little oil to coat the surface.
   - Dip each slice of bread into the egg mixture, allowing it to soak for about 20-30 seconds on each side until it is well coated but not falling apart.
4. **Cook the French Toast:**
   - Place the soaked bread slices onto the hot skillet or griddle.
   - Cook for 2-3 minutes on each side, or until golden brown and cooked through.
5. **Serve:**
   - Remove the French Toast from the skillet and place on a serving plate.
   - Dust with powdered sugar and serve with maple syrup, fresh berries, or any other toppings of your choice.

Tips:

- Use day-old bread for the best texture, as it will soak up the egg mixture without becoming too mushy.
- Adjust the sweetness to your preference by adding more or less sugar.
- You can customize your Pain Perdu with cinnamon, nutmeg, or other spices for extra flavor.

Enjoy your homemade Pain Perdu!

Pot-au-Feu (Beef Stew)

Ingredients:

- 2 lbs (about 1 kg) beef chuck roast, cut into large chunks
- 2-3 marrow bones (optional, for extra flavor)
- 2 onions, peeled and halved
- 4-5 carrots, peeled and cut into large chunks
- 3-4 celery stalks, cut into large chunks
- 2 leeks, white and light green parts only, cleaned and cut into large chunks
- 1 bouquet garni (a bundle of herbs such as parsley, thyme, and bay leaves tied together)
- Salt and freshly ground black pepper
- Water, enough to cover everything in the pot

Optional Accompaniments:

- Small potatoes, peeled and left whole
- Cabbage, cut into wedges
- Dijon mustard
- Cornichons or pickles
- Crusty bread

Instructions:

1. **Prepare the Ingredients:**
   - Tie the bouquet garni together with kitchen twine.
   - Cut the beef chuck roast into large chunks, and prepare the vegetables as indicated.
2. **Cooking the Pot-au-Feu:**
   - In a large stockpot or Dutch oven, place the beef chunks and marrow bones (if using).
   - Arrange the halved onions on top, and then add the bouquet garni.
   - Arrange the carrots, celery, and leeks around and on top of the beef.
   - Season generously with salt and pepper.
3. **Cooking the Stew:**
   - Pour enough water into the pot to cover all the ingredients.
   - Bring the pot to a gentle simmer over medium heat.
   - Skim any foam or impurities that rise to the surface.
4. **Simmering:**
   - Reduce the heat to low to maintain a gentle simmer.
   - Cover the pot partially with a lid, leaving some space for steam to escape.
   - Let the stew simmer for about 2.5 to 3 hours, or until the beef is very tender and the vegetables are cooked through.
5. **Adjust Seasoning and Serve:**

- Taste the broth and adjust the seasoning with salt and pepper if needed.
- Remove the bouquet garni and any marrow bones from the pot.
- Serve the Pot-au-Feu in bowls, with the beef and vegetables arranged nicely.
- You can serve with Dijon mustard on the side, and accompany with small potatoes, cabbage wedges, and cornichons if desired.
- Enjoy with crusty bread to soak up the delicious broth.

Tips:

- Pot-au-Feu is often served family-style, with the broth served as a first course and the meat and vegetables as the main course.
- Marrow bones add richness to the broth; if you can't find marrow bones, the stew will still be delicious without them.
- Adjust the vegetables and herbs according to your preference; some variations include adding turnips, parsnips, or different herbs like rosemary.

This hearty Pot-au-Feu is a wonderful dish to enjoy on a chilly day, bringing the flavors of classic French cooking to your table.

Salade Lyonnaise

Ingredients:

- 4 cups frisée lettuce or other bitter greens, torn into bite-sized pieces
- 100g bacon, cut into small strips (lardons)
- 2 large eggs
- 1 tablespoon white wine vinegar
- 1 teaspoon Dijon mustard
- 3 tablespoons olive oil
- Salt and freshly ground black pepper
- 1/2 cup croutons (optional)
- 1 shallot, finely chopped (optional)
- Chopped fresh parsley for garnish (optional)

Instructions:

1. **Prepare the Salad Greens:**
   - Wash and tear the frisée lettuce into bite-sized pieces. If using other bitter greens like curly endive or escarole, prepare them similarly.
2. **Cook the Bacon:**
   - In a skillet over medium heat, cook the bacon lardons until they are crispy and browned. Remove from the skillet and drain on paper towels.
3. **Make the Poached Eggs:**
   - Bring a pot of water to a gentle simmer. Add the white wine vinegar to the water.
   - Crack each egg into a small bowl or cup.
   - Create a gentle whirlpool in the simmering water and carefully slide each egg into the center of the whirlpool. Poach for about 3 minutes for a soft yolk.
   - Remove the poached eggs with a slotted spoon and place them on a plate lined with paper towels to drain excess water.
4. **Prepare the Vinaigrette:**
   - In a small bowl, whisk together the Dijon mustard, olive oil, and a pinch of salt and pepper. Adjust seasoning to taste. You can also add finely chopped shallots for extra flavor.
5. **Assemble the Salad:**
   - In a large bowl, toss the frisée lettuce with the vinaigrette until well coated.
   - Divide the dressed lettuce onto individual plates or bowls.
   - Arrange the crispy bacon lardons evenly over the salads.
   - Place a poached egg on top of each salad.
6. **Serve:**
   - Garnish the Salade Lyonnaise with croutons (if using) and chopped fresh parsley for added texture and flavor.
   - Serve immediately while the poached eggs are warm, allowing the yolk to mix with the vinaigrette and create a creamy dressing.

Tips:

- The key to a successful Salade Lyonnaise is balancing the bitterness of the greens with the richness of the egg and bacon. If you prefer less bitterness, you can mix frisée with other milder greens.
- Make sure the poached eggs are cooked to your desired level of doneness; a slightly runny yolk is traditional.
- Serve the salad with crusty French bread or a baguette to soak up any remaining egg yolk and vinaigrette.

Enjoy this classic French salad as a light and flavorful appetizer or a satisfying main course!

Clafoutis (Cherry Flan)

Ingredients:

- 1 cup fresh cherries, pitted (you can leave the pits in for a more traditional flavor, but warn eaters)
- 2/3 cup all-purpose flour
- 1/2 cup granulated sugar
- Pinch of salt
- 3 large eggs
- 1 cup milk
- 1/2 cup heavy cream
- 1 teaspoon vanilla extract
- Powdered sugar, for dusting

Instructions:

1. **Prepare the Cherries:**
   - Wash and pit the cherries. If you prefer, you can leave the pits in for a more traditional Clafoutis flavor, but make sure to warn those eating it.
2. **Preheat the Oven:**
   - Preheat your oven to 350°F (175°C). Butter a 9-inch (23 cm) round baking dish.
3. **Make the Batter:**
   - In a mixing bowl, whisk together the flour, granulated sugar, and salt.
   - In another bowl, whisk the eggs until smooth. Add the milk, heavy cream, and vanilla extract, and whisk until well combined.
   - Gradually add the wet ingredients to the dry ingredients, whisking constantly until the batter is smooth and free of lumps.
4. **Assemble the Clafoutis:**
   - Arrange the pitted cherries in the buttered baking dish in a single layer.
   - Pour the batter over the cherries, distributing it evenly.
5. **Bake the Clafoutis:**
   - Place the baking dish in the preheated oven and bake for 45-50 minutes, or until the Clafoutis is puffed up and golden brown on top, and a toothpick inserted into the center comes out clean.
6. **Serve:**
   - Remove the Clafoutis from the oven and let it cool slightly.
   - Dust the top with powdered sugar before serving.
   - Clafoutis can be served warm or at room temperature. It's delicious on its own or with a dollop of whipped cream or a scoop of vanilla ice cream.

Tips:

- You can experiment with other fruits such as berries, plums, or apricots in place of cherries.
- Traditional recipes often leave the pits in the cherries to impart a slight almond flavor, but it's perfectly fine to pit them if you prefer.
- The texture of Clafoutis should be between a custard and a cake, with a slightly dense consistency.

Enjoy this delightful Cherry Clafoutis as a perfect ending to a French-inspired meal, or as a sweet treat any time of day!

Rillettes de Porc (Pork Rillettes)

Ingredients:

- 2 lbs (about 900g) pork belly, skin removed and cut into cubes
- 1 lb (about 450g) pork shoulder, cut into cubes
- 2 cloves garlic, minced
- 1 bay leaf
- 1 teaspoon dried thyme
- 1 teaspoon dried rosemary
- Salt and freshly ground black pepper
- 1 cup water
- Pork fat (or duck fat) for cooking and preserving
- Baguette or crusty bread, for serving

Instructions:

1. **Prepare the Pork:**
    - In a large Dutch oven or heavy-bottomed pot, combine the pork belly and pork shoulder cubes.
    - Season generously with salt and pepper.
    - Add the minced garlic, bay leaf, dried thyme, and dried rosemary to the pot.
2. **Cook the Pork:**
    - Pour in enough water to barely cover the pork (about 1 cup).
    - Bring to a boil over medium-high heat, then reduce the heat to low and let it simmer gently, partially covered, for about 2.5 to 3 hours. Stir occasionally and add more water if needed to keep the meat from drying out.
3. **Shred the Pork:**
    - Once the pork is very tender and falling apart, remove it from the pot using a slotted spoon and transfer it to a large bowl.
    - Using two forks or a potato masher, shred the pork into small pieces. Discard any large pieces of fat or connective tissue that haven't rendered down.
4. **Season and Pack:**
    - Taste the shredded pork and adjust the seasoning with more salt and pepper if needed.
    - Pack the shredded pork tightly into clean jars or ramekins, pressing down firmly to remove any air pockets.
5. **Preserve with Fat:**
    - Melt the pork fat (or duck fat) in a small saucepan over low heat until it becomes liquid.
    - Pour the melted fat over the packed pork in the jars or ramekins, ensuring the meat is completely covered. This layer of fat acts as a seal and helps preserve the rillettes.

- Let the rillettes cool to room temperature, then cover with plastic wrap or lids and refrigerate for at least 4 hours, preferably overnight, to allow the flavors to meld.
6. **Serve:**
    - Before serving, remove the rillettes from the refrigerator and let them come to room temperature.
    - Serve the Pork Rillettes spread on slices of baguette or crusty bread.

Tips:

- Rillettes can be stored in the refrigerator for up to a week, tightly sealed with the fat layer intact.
- To serve, you can garnish with a sprinkle of fresh herbs like parsley or chives, or with cornichons (pickles) on the side for added flavor.
- Pork rillettes are best enjoyed at room temperature, where the flavors and textures are at their peak.

Enjoy your homemade Pork Rillettes as a delightful appetizer or snack, perfect for sharing with friends and family!

Boucheés à la Reine (Vol-au-Vents)

Ingredients:

For the Vol-au-Vents:

- 1 package (about 10 oz or 280g) frozen puff pastry sheets, thawed
- 1 egg, beaten (for egg wash)

For the Filling:

- 2 chicken breasts, cooked and diced
- 200g mushrooms, sliced
- 2 tablespoons butter
- 2 tablespoons all-purpose flour
- 1 cup chicken broth
- 1/2 cup heavy cream
- 1 tablespoon lemon juice
- Salt and pepper, to taste
- Fresh parsley, chopped (for garnish)

Instructions:

1. **Prepare the Vol-au-Vents:**
    - Preheat your oven to 400°F (200°C).
    - Roll out the thawed puff pastry sheets on a lightly floured surface to about 1/4 inch thickness.
    - Using a round cutter or glass, cut out circles of dough. You can choose the size depending on whether you want small bite-sized bouchées or larger ones.
    - Using a smaller cutter or glass, make an indentation about 1/2 inch inside each circle without cutting all the way through (this will create the top layer).
    - Place the rounds on a baking sheet lined with parchment paper.
    - Brush the tops with beaten egg to create a shiny finish.
    - Bake in the preheated oven for about 15-20 minutes, or until the pastry is puffed and golden brown. Remove from the oven and let cool on a wire rack.
2. **Prepare the Filling:**
    - In a large skillet, melt the butter over medium heat.
    - Add the sliced mushrooms and cook until they are softened and browned, about 5-7 minutes.
    - Remove the mushrooms from the skillet and set aside.
    - In the same skillet, add a bit more butter if needed. Stir in the flour to create a roux, cooking for about 1-2 minutes to remove the raw flour taste.
    - Gradually whisk in the chicken broth, stirring constantly to avoid lumps.
    - Cook the sauce until it thickens, then reduce the heat to low.
    - Stir in the heavy cream and lemon juice. Season with salt and pepper to taste.

- Add the cooked diced chicken and mushrooms back into the skillet, stirring gently to combine and heat through.
3. **Assemble the Bouchées à la Reine:**
    - Carefully remove the top layer of each baked puff pastry shell.
    - Spoon the creamy chicken and mushroom filling into the hollowed-out shells.
    - Replace the top layer of pastry on each shell.
    - Garnish with chopped fresh parsley.
4. **Serve:**
    - Bouchées à la Reine are traditionally served warm. Arrange them on a serving platter and enjoy immediately.

Tips:

- You can prepare the puff pastry shells in advance and store them in an airtight container at room temperature. Reheat them in the oven briefly before filling to ensure they are crisp.
- Feel free to customize the filling with other ingredients such as seafood or vegetables.
- These elegant Vol-au-Vents make a perfect appetizer for special occasions or a delightful main dish paired with a salad.

Enjoy creating these delicious and elegant Bouchées à la Reine at home, bringing a taste of classic French cuisine to your table!

Boudin Blanc (White Sausage)

Ingredients:

- 1 lb (450g) boneless, skinless chicken thighs (or use a combination of chicken and pork/veal)
- 1/2 cup milk
- 1/2 cup heavy cream
- 1/2 cup fresh breadcrumbs
- 1 small onion, finely chopped
- 1/4 teaspoon ground nutmeg
- 1/4 teaspoon ground white pepper
- Salt, to taste
- Pork casings (optional)
- Butter or oil, for cooking

Instructions:

1. **Prepare the Meat:**
   - Cut the chicken thighs (and any additional meats if using) into small pieces.
2. **Make the Sausage Mixture:**
   - In a bowl, combine the chicken pieces, milk, heavy cream, breadcrumbs, chopped onion, ground nutmeg, ground white pepper, and salt.
   - Mix well until everything is evenly combined and the mixture becomes slightly sticky.
3. **Forming the Sausage:**
   - If using casings, rinse them thoroughly in cold water and soak them in warm water to soften.
   - Stuff the sausage mixture into the casings using a sausage stuffer or a piping bag fitted with a large tip. Tie off the ends with kitchen twine and twist into links if desired.
   - If not using casings, shape the mixture into sausage-like shapes with your hands, about 4-6 inches long.
4. **Cooking:**
   - Heat a large skillet over medium heat and add butter or oil.
   - Cook the sausages until they are golden brown on all sides and cooked through, about 15-20 minutes depending on size. Make sure the internal temperature reaches 165°F (74°C).
5. **Serving:**
   - Serve the Boudin Blanc hot, accompanied by mustard, mashed potatoes, or a side salad.

Tips:

- If you prefer a smoother texture, you can blend the meat mixture in a food processor before stuffing into casings.
- Boudin Blanc can also be poached in simmering water or broth until cooked through, then browned in a skillet for added color and flavor.
- Adjust the spices and seasoning according to your taste preferences.

Enjoy making and savoring this classic French sausage, Boudin Blanc, whether for a special occasion or a delicious meal any time!

Poulet Basquaise (Basque Chicken)

Ingredients:

- 4 chicken thighs, bone-in and skin-on
- 4 chicken drumsticks, bone-in and skin-on
- Salt and freshly ground black pepper
- 2 tablespoons olive oil
- 1 onion, finely chopped
- 2 garlic cloves, minced
- 1 red bell pepper, sliced
- 1 green bell pepper, sliced
- 1 yellow bell pepper, sliced
- 1 can (14 oz / 400g) diced tomatoes
- 1/2 cup chicken broth
- 1/4 cup dry white wine (optional)
- 1 teaspoon paprika
- 1/2 teaspoon dried thyme
- Pinch of cayenne pepper (optional, for heat)
- Chopped fresh parsley, for garnish

Instructions:

1. **Season and Brown the Chicken:**
    - Season the chicken thighs and drumsticks generously with salt and pepper.
    - Heat the olive oil in a large skillet or Dutch oven over medium-high heat.
    - Brown the chicken pieces on all sides until golden brown, about 4-5 minutes per side. Remove from the skillet and set aside.
2. **Cook the Vegetables:**
    - In the same skillet or Dutch oven, add the chopped onion and cook until softened, about 3-4 minutes.
    - Add the minced garlic and cook for another 1 minute until fragrant.
    - Add the sliced bell peppers and cook for 5-6 minutes until they begin to soften.
3. **Add Tomatoes and Liquid:**
    - Stir in the diced tomatoes with their juices.
    - Add the chicken broth and white wine (if using), stirring to combine.
    - Season with paprika, dried thyme, and cayenne pepper (if using).
    - Bring the mixture to a simmer.
4. **Braise the Chicken:**
    - Return the browned chicken pieces to the skillet, nestling them into the vegetable mixture.
    - Cover the skillet or Dutch oven with a lid, reduce the heat to low, and let simmer gently for 30-35 minutes, or until the chicken is cooked through and tender. Stir occasionally and add more broth if needed to keep the sauce from drying out.

5. **Serve:**
    - Once the chicken is cooked through and the sauce has thickened slightly, taste and adjust seasoning with salt and pepper if needed.
    - Serve Poulet Basquaise hot, garnished with chopped fresh parsley.

Tips:

- You can add spicy chorizo sausage slices along with the bell peppers for extra flavor.
- Poulet Basquaise is traditionally served with rice, pasta, or crusty bread to soak up the delicious sauce.
- For a richer sauce, you can add a tablespoon of tomato paste along with the diced tomatoes.

Enjoy preparing and savoring this hearty and aromatic Poulet Basquaise, bringing the flavors of the Basque region of France to your table!

Far Breton (Prune Cake)

Ingredients:

- 1 cup (150g) pitted prunes
- 3/4 cup (100g) all-purpose flour
- 1/2 cup (100g) granulated sugar
- Pinch of salt
- 3 large eggs
- 2 cups (500ml) whole milk
- 1 teaspoon vanilla extract
- Butter, for greasing the pan
- Powdered sugar, for dusting (optional)

Instructions:

1. **Prepare the Prunes:**
   - Place the prunes in a small bowl and cover them with hot water. Let them soak for about 10 minutes to soften. Drain well and set aside.
2. **Preheat the Oven:**
   - Preheat your oven to 350°F (175°C).
   - Butter a 9-inch (23cm) round baking dish or cake pan.
3. **Prepare the Batter:**
   - In a large bowl, whisk together the flour, granulated sugar, and salt.
   - In another bowl, whisk the eggs until smooth.
   - Gradually add the milk and vanilla extract to the eggs, whisking constantly.
4. **Combine and Bake:**
   - Gradually add the wet ingredients to the dry ingredients, whisking until the batter is smooth and free of lumps.
   - Fold in the drained prunes.
5. **Bake the Far Breton:**
   - Pour the batter into the prepared baking dish.
   - Bake in the preheated oven for 45-55 minutes, or until the Far Breton is set and golden brown on top. It should be firm to the touch but still slightly jiggly in the center.
6. **Cool and Serve:**
   - Remove from the oven and let the Far Breton cool in the pan for about 10 minutes.
   - Transfer to a wire rack to cool completely.
   - Dust with powdered sugar before serving, if desired.

Tips:

- Far Breton is best served at room temperature or slightly warm.

- You can vary the fruit used in Far Breton; traditional versions use prunes, but you can also try it with dried cherries or apricots.
- Some variations include adding a splash of dark rum or Armagnac to the batter for extra flavor.

Enjoy this classic French dessert, Far Breton, with its rich custardy texture and sweet prunes—a perfect treat for any occasion!

Brioche

Ingredients:

- 3 cups (375g) all-purpose flour
- 1/4 cup (50g) granulated sugar
- 1 teaspoon salt
- 1 packet (7g or 2 1/4 teaspoons) active dry yeast
- 1/4 cup (60ml) warm milk
- 3 large eggs, room temperature
- 1/2 cup (115g) unsalted butter, softened, plus extra for greasing

Optional Egg Wash:

- 1 egg, beaten

Instructions:

1. **Activate the Yeast:**
   - In a small bowl, dissolve the yeast and a pinch of sugar in the warm milk. Let it sit for about 5-10 minutes until frothy.
2. **Mix the Dough:**
   - In a large mixing bowl or the bowl of a stand mixer fitted with the dough hook attachment, combine the flour, sugar, and salt.
   - Make a well in the center and add the yeast mixture and eggs.
3. **Knead the Dough:**
   - Mix the ingredients until they come together to form a dough. If using a stand mixer, knead on medium speed for about 5 minutes until the dough becomes smooth and elastic.
   - Gradually add the softened butter, a few pieces at a time, while continuing to knead until all the butter is fully incorporated and the dough is smooth and shiny. This process can take about 10-15 minutes.
4. **First Rise:**
   - Shape the dough into a ball and place it in a greased bowl. Cover with a clean kitchen towel or plastic wrap and let it rise in a warm place for 1-2 hours, or until doubled in size.
5. **Shape the Brioche:**
   - Punch down the risen dough to deflate it and transfer it to a lightly floured surface.
   - Divide the dough into portions and shape them into balls or into a loaf, depending on your preference. You can use a brioche mold for a classic shape.
   - Place the shaped dough into greased pans or molds.
6. **Second Rise:**

- Cover the pans or molds with a clean kitchen towel or plastic wrap and let the dough rise again in a warm place for another 1-2 hours, or until doubled in size.
7. **Bake the Brioche:**
    - Preheat your oven to 375°F (190°C).
    - If using, brush the top of the brioche with beaten egg for a shiny finish.
    - Bake the brioche for 20-25 minutes (for smaller portions) to 35-40 minutes (for larger loaves), or until golden brown on top and cooked through. The internal temperature should reach about 190°F (88°C) on an instant-read thermometer.
8. **Cool and Serve:**
    - Remove the brioche from the oven and let it cool in the pans for a few minutes before transferring to a wire rack to cool completely.
    - Slice and serve the brioche warm or at room temperature. It's delicious on its own, with butter, or as a base for sandwiches or French toast.

Tips:

- Brioche can be stored at room temperature for a day or two, but it's best enjoyed fresh. You can also freeze it for longer storage.
- Customize your brioche by adding raisins, chocolate chips, or candied fruits to the dough during the mixing process.
- For a richer flavor, you can replace some of the milk with cream.

Enjoy the process of making this classic French bread, Brioche, and savor its buttery, tender texture with every bite!

Pissaladière (Onion Tart)

Ingredients:

For the Dough:

- 2 cups (250g) all-purpose flour
- 1 teaspoon salt
- 1 teaspoon sugar
- 1 packet (7g or 2 1/4 teaspoons) active dry yeast
- 3/4 cup (180ml) warm water
- 2 tablespoons olive oil

For the Topping:

- 4 large yellow onions, thinly sliced
- 3 tablespoons olive oil
- 1 teaspoon dried thyme (or fresh thyme leaves)
- Salt and freshly ground black pepper, to taste
- 12-15 black olives, pitted and halved
- 6-8 anchovy fillets, drained (optional)
- Fresh thyme leaves, for garnish (optional)

Instructions:

1. **Prepare the Dough:**
   - In a large bowl, combine the flour, salt, and sugar. Mix well.
   - In a small bowl, dissolve the yeast in warm water. Let it sit for 5-10 minutes until frothy.
   - Add the olive oil to the yeast mixture.
   - Make a well in the center of the flour mixture and pour in the yeast mixture.
   - Stir until the dough comes together.
   - Turn the dough out onto a floured surface and knead for about 5-7 minutes, until smooth and elastic.
   - Place the dough in a lightly oiled bowl, cover with a clean kitchen towel or plastic wrap, and let it rise in a warm place for about 1 hour, or until doubled in size.
2. **Prepare the Onion Topping:**
   - While the dough is rising, heat 3 tablespoons of olive oil in a large skillet over medium heat.
   - Add the thinly sliced onions and cook, stirring occasionally, until they are caramelized and golden brown, about 30-40 minutes.
   - Stir in the dried thyme (or fresh thyme leaves) and season with salt and pepper to taste. Remove from heat and set aside.
3. **Assemble and Bake the Pissaladière:**
   - Preheat your oven to 400°F (200°C).

- Punch down the risen dough and roll it out on a lightly floured surface to fit a baking sheet or tart pan (about 9x13 inches or 23x33 cm).
- Transfer the rolled-out dough to a lightly greased baking sheet or tart pan.
- Spread the caramelized onion mixture evenly over the dough, leaving a small border around the edges.
- Arrange the halved black olives and anchovy fillets (if using) on top of the onions in a decorative pattern.
- Drizzle a little extra olive oil over the top.

4. **Bake the Pissaladière:**
   - Place the Pissaladière in the preheated oven and bake for 20-25 minutes, or until the crust is golden brown and cooked through.
   - Remove from the oven and let it cool slightly before slicing.

5. **Serve:**
   - Garnish with fresh thyme leaves, if desired.
   - Cut into squares or wedges and serve warm or at room temperature.

Tips:

- Pissaladière is traditionally served as an appetizer or light meal, often accompanied by a glass of wine.
- You can customize the toppings by adding roasted garlic, cherry tomatoes, or even cheese like goat cheese or Gruyère.
- Leftovers can be stored in an airtight container in the refrigerator for a few days and reheated gently in the oven before serving.

Enjoy making and savoring this classic French Onion Tart, Pissaladière, with its rich flavors of caramelized onions and savory toppings!

Madeleines

Ingredients:

- 2/3 cup (135g) granulated sugar
- Zest of 1 lemon (or 1 teaspoon vanilla extract)
- 3 large eggs, at room temperature
- 1 cup (125g) all-purpose flour
- 1 teaspoon baking powder
- 1/4 teaspoon salt
- 10 tablespoons (140g) unsalted butter, melted and cooled
- Additional melted butter and flour, for preparing the molds

Instructions:

1. **Prepare the Madeleine Molds:**
   - Brush the indentations of a madeleine mold with melted butter. Dust with flour, tap off any excess flour, and refrigerate the mold while preparing the batter.
2. **Prepare the Batter:**
   - In a mixing bowl, combine the granulated sugar and lemon zest (or vanilla extract). Rub together with your fingers to release the oils from the zest and infuse the sugar.
   - Add the eggs to the sugar mixture and whisk until pale and thickened, about 5 minutes with a hand mixer or 2-3 minutes with a stand mixer fitted with the whisk attachment.
3. **Fold in Dry Ingredients:**
   - In a separate bowl, sift together the flour, baking powder, and salt.
   - Gradually fold the flour mixture into the egg mixture using a spatula, a third at a time, until just incorporated.
4. **Add Melted Butter:**
   - Gently fold in the melted butter until fully incorporated into the batter.
5. **Rest the Batter:**
   - Cover the bowl with plastic wrap and refrigerate for at least 1 hour, or up to overnight. This resting period helps the batter develop and ensures the characteristic hump of madeleines.
6. **Bake the Madeleines:**
   - Preheat your oven to 375°F (190°C).
   - Spoon the batter into the prepared madeleine molds, filling each mold about 3/4 full.
7. **Bake:**
   - Bake in the preheated oven for 10-12 minutes, or until the edges are golden brown and the centers spring back when lightly touched.
8. **Cool and Serve:**

- Remove from the oven and immediately tap the madeleine mold against a hard surface to release the madeleines.
- Transfer the madeleines to a wire rack to cool completely.

Tips:

- Madeleines are best enjoyed fresh on the day they are made. They have a delicate texture and are perfect with tea or coffee.
- You can vary the flavor by adding different zests (orange, lime) or spices (such as ground cinnamon or cardamom).
- If you don't have a madeleine mold, you can use mini muffin pans, though the shape will be different.

Enjoy baking and indulging in these delightful French Madeleines, whether as a treat for yourself or to impress guests with your baking skills!

Tartiflette (Potato, Reblochon Cheese, and Bacon Dish)

Ingredients:

- 2 lbs (about 1 kg) potatoes (Yukon Gold or similar), peeled and sliced into 1/4-inch thick rounds
- 1 tablespoon butter
- 1 tablespoon olive oil
- 1 large onion, thinly sliced
- 6 oz (170g) lardons (thick-cut bacon or pancetta), diced
- 1/2 cup (120ml) dry white wine (optional)
- Salt and freshly ground black pepper, to taste
- 1 whole reblochon cheese (about 1 lb or 450g), sliced in half horizontally
- Fresh thyme leaves, for garnish (optional)

Instructions:

1. **Prepare the Potatoes:**
   - Place the sliced potatoes in a large pot of salted water. Bring to a boil and cook for about 5-7 minutes, until just tender. Drain and set aside.
2. **Cook the Lardons and Onions:**
   - In a large skillet, heat the butter and olive oil over medium heat.
   - Add the diced lardons (bacon or pancetta) and cook until they start to crisp up, about 5-7 minutes.
   - Add the thinly sliced onions to the skillet and cook until they are softened and golden brown, about 8-10 minutes.
   - If using, pour in the white wine and cook for another 2-3 minutes, allowing the alcohol to evaporate. Season with salt and pepper to taste.
3. **Assemble the Tartiflette:**
   - Preheat your oven to 375°F (190°C).
   - Grease a baking dish (approximately 9x13 inches or similar size).
   - Arrange half of the cooked potatoes in the bottom of the baking dish.
   - Spread half of the onion and lardon mixture evenly over the potatoes.
   - Place half of the reblochon cheese, rind side up, on top of the onion and lardon mixture.
   - Repeat with the remaining potatoes, onion and lardon mixture, and reblochon cheese.
4. **Bake the Tartiflette:**
   - Bake in the preheated oven for 20-25 minutes, or until the cheese is melted and bubbly, and the top is golden brown.
5. **Serve:**
   - Remove from the oven and let it cool slightly before serving.
   - Garnish with fresh thyme leaves if desired.
   - Serve Tartiflette warm, scooping out portions directly from the baking dish.

Tips:

- Reblochon cheese is traditional for Tartiflette, but if you can't find it, you can use a similar creamy and slightly tangy cheese like Époisses or a mix of Gruyère and Brie.
- You can adjust the amount of lardons and onions based on your preference for a more bacon-forward or milder flavor.
- Tartiflette is often served with a crisp green salad and pairs well with a glass of white wine or a light red wine.

Enjoy this comforting and flavorful Tartiflette, perfect for a cozy dinner or après-ski meal, bringing the flavors of the French Alps to your table!

Moules Marinières (Mussels in White Wine)

Ingredients:

- 2 lbs (about 1 kg) fresh mussels
- 2 tablespoons unsalted butter
- 2 tablespoons olive oil
- 2 shallots, finely chopped
- 2 cloves garlic, minced
- 1 cup dry white wine (such as Sauvignon Blanc or Pinot Grigio)
- 1/2 cup heavy cream (optional, for a creamy version)
- Salt and freshly ground black pepper, to taste
- 1/4 cup chopped fresh parsley
- Crusty bread, for serving

Instructions:

1. **Prepare the Mussels:**
    - Scrub the mussels under cold running water, removing any beards (fibrous threads) and discarding any mussels that are cracked or open and do not close when tapped lightly.
2. **Cook the Shallots and Garlic:**
    - In a large pot or Dutch oven, heat the butter and olive oil over medium heat.
    - Add the finely chopped shallots and minced garlic. Cook, stirring frequently, until softened and fragrant, about 3-4 minutes.
3. **Add the Mussels:**
    - Increase the heat to medium-high. Pour in the white wine and bring to a boil.
    - Add the cleaned mussels to the pot. Cover with a lid and cook for 5-7 minutes, shaking the pot occasionally, until the mussels have opened. Discard any mussels that do not open.
4. **Finish the Dish:**
    - If using heavy cream, stir it into the broth after the mussels have cooked and opened. Season with salt and pepper to taste.
    - Stir in the chopped parsley, reserving some for garnish.
5. **Serve:**
    - Ladle the mussels and broth into serving bowls.
    - Garnish with additional chopped parsley.
    - Serve immediately with crusty bread to soak up the delicious broth.

Tips:

- Serve Moules Marinières as a main course with French fries (traditional Belgian style) or as a starter.

- Make sure to discard any mussels that do not open after cooking, as they may not be safe to eat.
- For a lighter version, you can omit the cream and enjoy the mussels with just the white wine broth.

Enjoy preparing and savoring this classic French seafood dish, Moules Marinières, which highlights the delicate flavor of mussels in a delightful white wine and garlic broth!

Crêpes Suzette

Ingredients:

For the Crêpes:

- 1 cup (125g) all-purpose flour
- 2 tablespoons granulated sugar
- Pinch of salt
- 3 large eggs
- 1 1/4 cups (300ml) milk
- 2 tablespoons unsalted butter, melted
- Butter or oil, for cooking the crêpes

For the Sauce:

- 1/2 cup (100g) granulated sugar
- Zest of 1 orange
- Juice of 2 oranges (about 1 cup or 240ml)
- 4 tablespoons (55g) unsalted butter, cubed
- 1/4 cup (60ml) Grand Marnier or orange liqueur
- Additional Grand Marnier or Cognac, for flambéing (optional)

To Serve:

- Vanilla ice cream or whipped cream (optional)
- Fresh orange segments, for garnish (optional)

Instructions:

1. **Prepare the Crêpe Batter:**
   - In a large mixing bowl, whisk together the flour, sugar, and salt.
   - Make a well in the center and add the eggs. Whisk the eggs into the flour mixture.
   - Gradually add the milk, whisking constantly, until the batter is smooth and free of lumps.
   - Whisk in the melted butter until well combined.
   - Let the batter rest for about 30 minutes at room temperature.
2. **Cook the Crêpes:**
   - Heat a non-stick skillet or crêpe pan over medium heat. Add a small amount of butter or oil and swirl to coat the pan evenly.
   - Pour a small ladleful of batter into the pan, tilting and swirling the pan to spread the batter thinly and evenly.
   - Cook the crêpe for about 1-2 minutes until the edges start to lift and the bottom is golden brown.

- Flip the crêpe and cook for another 1 minute until cooked through. Transfer to a plate and repeat with the remaining batter, stacking the crêpes as you go.

3. **Prepare the Sauce:**
   - In a large skillet or saucepan, combine the granulated sugar and orange zest. Cook over medium heat, stirring constantly, until the sugar melts and caramelizes to a golden brown color.
   - Carefully add the orange juice to the caramelized sugar (it will bubble up vigorously). Stir until the caramel has dissolved into the orange juice.
   - Reduce the heat to low and stir in the cubed butter until melted and fully incorporated into the sauce.
   - Stir in the Grand Marnier or orange liqueur. Let the sauce simmer for a few minutes until slightly thickened.

4. **Assemble Crêpes Suzette:**
   - Fold each crêpe into quarters and place them in the skillet with the sauce, coating them evenly with the sauce.
   - If desired, carefully ignite the sauce with a match or lighter (optional step for flambéing). Be cautious when doing this and keep a lid nearby to extinguish the flame if necessary.
   - Serve the Crêpes Suzette immediately while still warm.

5. **To Serve:**
   - Arrange the Crêpes Suzette on serving plates.
   - Optionally, top each serving with a scoop of vanilla ice cream or whipped cream.
   - Garnish with fresh orange segments if desired.

Tips:

- The crêpes can be made ahead and stored stacked with parchment paper in between to prevent sticking. Warm them gently in the skillet with the sauce before serving.
- Be cautious when flambéing the Crêpes Suzette. Ensure your kitchen is well-ventilated and keep a fire extinguisher or damp cloth nearby.
- The sauce should be served warm and immediately after preparation for the best flavor and texture.

Enjoy the process of making and serving this elegant French dessert, Crêpes Suzette, with its delightful combination of citrusy flavors and flambéed flair!

Blanquette de Veau (Veal Stew)

Ingredients:

- 2 lbs (about 1 kg) veal shoulder or stewing veal, cut into 1-inch cubes
- Salt and freshly ground black pepper, to taste
- 2 tablespoons unsalted butter
- 2 tablespoons vegetable oil
- 1 onion, diced
- 2 carrots, peeled and sliced
- 2 celery stalks, sliced
- 2 cloves garlic, minced
- 1 bay leaf
- 4-5 sprigs fresh thyme
- 1/4 cup (30g) all-purpose flour
- 3 cups (720ml) chicken or veal stock
- 1 cup (240ml) dry white wine
- 1 cup (240ml) heavy cream
- 1 tablespoon Dijon mustard (optional)
- 1 tablespoon lemon juice (optional)
- Chopped fresh parsley, for garnish

Instructions:

1. **Prepare the Veal:**
   - Season the veal cubes generously with salt and pepper.
   - In a large Dutch oven or heavy-bottomed pot, heat the butter and oil over medium-high heat.
   - Brown the veal cubes in batches, ensuring they are well-browned on all sides. Transfer the browned veal to a plate and set aside.
2. **Cook the Vegetables:**
   - In the same pot, add the diced onion, carrots, celery, and minced garlic. Cook, stirring occasionally, until the vegetables begin to soften, about 5-7 minutes.
3. **Create the Stew Base:**
   - Return the browned veal cubes to the pot with the vegetables.
   - Add the bay leaf and fresh thyme sprigs.
   - Sprinkle the flour over the meat and vegetables, stirring to coat everything evenly.
   - Cook for 2-3 minutes to cook off the raw flour taste.
4. **Simmer the Stew:**
   - Pour in the chicken or veal stock and white wine, stirring to combine and scraping any browned bits from the bottom of the pot.

- Bring the mixture to a simmer, then reduce the heat to low. Cover and simmer gently for 1.5 to 2 hours, or until the veal is tender and cooked through. Stir occasionally.

5. **Finish the Blanquette:**
   - Once the veal is tender, stir in the heavy cream.
   - Optionally, stir in the Dijon mustard and lemon juice for added flavor (if using).
   - Simmer gently for another 10-15 minutes to allow the flavors to meld and the sauce to thicken slightly. Adjust seasoning with salt and pepper if needed.
6. **Serve:**
   - Remove the bay leaf and thyme sprigs.
   - Garnish with chopped fresh parsley before serving.
   - Blanquette de Veau is traditionally served hot, accompanied by rice, boiled potatoes, or crusty bread.

Tips:

- For a richer sauce, you can add a couple of egg yolks mixed with a bit of cream just before serving (be careful not to curdle the sauce).
- Blanquette de Veau is even better when prepared a day ahead, as the flavors have more time to meld together. Simply reheat gently before serving.
- This dish pairs beautifully with a crisp white wine, such as Chardonnay or Sauvignon Blanc.

Enjoy preparing and savoring this classic French veal stew, Blanquette de Veau, with its creamy sauce and tender pieces of veal—a true comfort food that delights with every bite!

Gratin de Pommes de Terre (Potato Gratin)

Ingredients:

- 2 lbs (about 1 kg) Yukon Gold potatoes, peeled and thinly sliced (about 1/8 inch thick)
- 2 cups (480 ml) heavy cream
- 1 cup (240 ml) whole milk
- 2 cloves garlic, minced
- 1 bay leaf
- 1/4 teaspoon freshly grated nutmeg
- Salt and freshly ground black pepper, to taste
- 1 1/2 cups (150g) grated Gruyère cheese (or Swiss cheese)
- 1/2 cup (50g) grated Parmesan cheese
- Butter, for greasing the baking dish
- Chopped fresh parsley, for garnish (optional)

Instructions:

1. **Preheat the Oven:**
   - Preheat your oven to 375°F (190°C). Butter a 9x13-inch (23x33 cm) baking dish or a similar-sized gratin dish.
2. **Prepare the Potatoes:**
   - Peel the potatoes and slice them thinly, about 1/8 inch thick. You can use a mandoline slicer for even slices.
3. **Make the Cream Mixture:**
   - In a saucepan, combine the heavy cream, milk, minced garlic, bay leaf, nutmeg, salt, and pepper. Heat over medium heat until it just begins to simmer. Remove from heat and let infuse for about 10 minutes. Remove the bay leaf and garlic cloves.
4. **Assemble the Gratin:**
   - Arrange half of the sliced potatoes in the prepared baking dish, overlapping slightly.
   - Sprinkle half of the grated Gruyère cheese and Parmesan cheese over the potatoes.
   - Repeat with the remaining potatoes and cheeses.
5. **Pour the Cream Mixture:**
   - Carefully pour the infused cream mixture over the potatoes and cheese, ensuring that the potatoes are evenly covered.
6. **Bake the Gratin:**
   - Cover the baking dish with foil and bake in the preheated oven for 45 minutes.
7. **Brown the Top:**
   - After 45 minutes, remove the foil and continue baking for another 20-25 minutes, or until the potatoes are tender and the top is golden brown and bubbly.
8. **Serve:**

- Remove from the oven and let the Potato Gratin rest for a few minutes before serving.
- Garnish with chopped fresh parsley if desired.
- Serve hot as a delicious side dish to accompany roasted meats, poultry, or as a main dish with a crisp green salad.

Tips:

- You can customize the flavors by adding herbs like thyme or rosemary to the cream mixture.
- For a richer gratin, you can add a layer of crispy bacon or pancetta between the layers of potatoes and cheese.
- Leftovers can be stored in the refrigerator for a few days and reheated gently in the oven.

Enjoy making and savoring this creamy and comforting Potato Gratin, a perfect dish for any occasion that showcases the deliciousness of simple ingredients transformed into a luxurious treat!

Boeuf Bourguignon

Ingredients:

- 2 lbs (about 1 kg) beef chuck roast, cut into 1-inch cubes
- Salt and freshly ground black pepper, to taste
- 2 tablespoons all-purpose flour
- 4 tablespoons unsalted butter, divided
- 2 tablespoons olive oil
- 4 slices bacon, chopped
- 1 large onion, chopped
- 2 carrots, peeled and sliced
- 2 cloves garlic, minced
- 1 bouquet garni (a bundle of fresh herbs such as thyme, parsley, and bay leaf tied together with kitchen twine)
- 2 cups (480 ml) red wine (such as Burgundy, Pinot Noir, or Merlot)
- 2 cups (480 ml) beef broth
- 2 tablespoons tomato paste
- 1 tablespoon Worcestershire sauce (optional)
- 8 oz (225g) pearl onions, peeled (frozen pearl onions are convenient)
- 8 oz (225g) mushrooms, quartered (cremini or button mushrooms)
- Chopped fresh parsley, for garnish (optional)

Instructions:

1. **Prepare the Beef:**
   - Pat the beef cubes dry with paper towels and season generously with salt and pepper. Dredge the beef in flour, shaking off any excess.
2. **Brown the Beef:**
   - In a large Dutch oven or heavy-bottomed pot, heat 2 tablespoons of butter and olive oil over medium-high heat.
   - Add the beef cubes in batches and brown them on all sides. Do not overcrowd the pot to ensure proper browning. Transfer the browned beef to a plate and set aside.
3. **Cook the Bacon and Vegetables:**
   - In the same pot, add the chopped bacon and cook until crispy. Remove the bacon with a slotted spoon and set aside.
   - Add the chopped onion and sliced carrots to the pot. Cook, stirring occasionally, until softened, about 5-7 minutes.
   - Add the minced garlic and cook for another minute until fragrant.
4. **Deglaze the Pot:**
   - Return the browned beef cubes and crispy bacon to the pot.
   - Pour in the red wine, scraping the bottom of the pot to loosen any browned bits (this adds flavor to the stew).

- Add the beef broth, tomato paste, and Worcestershire sauce (if using). Stir to combine.
5. **Simmer the Stew:**
    - Add the bouquet garni (bundle of herbs tied together) to the pot.
    - Bring the stew to a simmer, then reduce the heat to low. Cover and simmer gently for 2 to 2.5 hours, stirring occasionally, until the beef is tender and the flavors have melded.
6. **Prepare the Pearl Onions and Mushrooms:**
    - While the stew is simmering, prepare the pearl onions and mushrooms.
    - In a separate skillet, melt the remaining 2 tablespoons of butter over medium heat.
    - Add the pearl onions and cook until they start to brown, about 8-10 minutes. Set aside.
    - In the same skillet, add the quartered mushrooms and cook until they are browned and tender, about 5-7 minutes. Set aside.
7. **Finish the Stew:**
    - Once the beef is tender, remove the bouquet garni from the pot.
    - Stir in the cooked pearl onions and mushrooms. Simmer for another 10-15 minutes to heat through and allow the flavors to meld.
    - Adjust seasoning with salt and pepper if needed.
8. **Serve:**
    - Ladle the Boeuf Bourguignon into serving bowls.
    - Garnish with chopped fresh parsley if desired.
    - Serve hot, accompanied by crusty bread, mashed potatoes, or over egg noodles.

Tips:

- Boeuf Bourguignon tastes even better the next day as the flavors continue to develop. It can be refrigerated for up to 3 days or frozen for longer storage.
- Serve this dish with a glass of the same red wine used in the recipe for a perfect pairing.
- Don't rush the browning step for the beef; it adds depth of flavor to the stew.

Enjoy preparing and savoring this iconic French dish, Boeuf Bourguignon, which combines tender beef, savory vegetables, and a rich wine-infused sauce for a truly comforting meal!

Normandy-style Chicken

Ingredients:

- 4 boneless, skinless chicken breasts
- Salt and freshly ground black pepper, to taste
- 2 tablespoons all-purpose flour
- 2 tablespoons unsalted butter
- 1 tablespoon olive oil
- 1 onion, thinly sliced
- 8 oz (225g) mushrooms, sliced
- 2 apples (such as Granny Smith or Braeburn), peeled, cored, and sliced
- 1/2 cup (120ml) apple cider or apple juice
- 1/2 cup (120ml) chicken broth
- 1/2 cup (120ml) heavy cream
- 1 tablespoon Dijon mustard
- 1 tablespoon chopped fresh thyme leaves
- Chopped fresh parsley, for garnish (optional)

Instructions:

1. **Prepare the Chicken:**
   - Season the chicken breasts with salt and pepper.
   - Dredge the chicken in flour, shaking off any excess.
2. **Cook the Chicken:**
   - In a large skillet, heat 1 tablespoon of butter and 1 tablespoon of olive oil over medium-high heat.
   - Add the chicken breasts and cook until golden brown on both sides and cooked through, about 4-5 minutes per side depending on thickness. Remove the chicken from the skillet and set aside.
3. **Cook the Vegetables and Apples:**
   - In the same skillet, add the remaining tablespoon of butter.
   - Add the sliced onion and cook until softened, about 3-4 minutes.
   - Add the sliced mushrooms and cook until they release their juices and begin to brown, about 5-6 minutes.
   - Add the sliced apples and cook for another 2-3 minutes until they start to soften.
4. **Make the Sauce:**
   - Pour in the apple cider (or apple juice) and chicken broth, scraping the bottom of the skillet to deglaze and pick up any browned bits.
   - Stir in the heavy cream, Dijon mustard, and chopped thyme leaves. Bring the sauce to a simmer and cook for 5-7 minutes until slightly thickened.
5. **Combine and Serve:**
   - Return the chicken breasts to the skillet, nestling them into the sauce and vegetables.

- Simmer gently for another 5 minutes to heat through and allow the flavors to meld.
- Garnish with chopped fresh parsley if desired.
6. **Serve:**
    - Serve the Normandy-style Chicken hot, spooning the creamy cider sauce, mushrooms, apples, and onions over each chicken breast.
    - It pairs well with rice, mashed potatoes, or crusty bread to soak up the delicious sauce.

Tips:

- Choose firm apples that hold their shape well when cooked, such as Granny Smith or Braeburn, for the best texture in the dish.
- Adjust the thickness of the sauce by simmering for longer if you prefer a thicker consistency.
- For added depth of flavor, you can deglaze the skillet with a splash of brandy or Calvados (apple brandy) before adding the cider and chicken broth.

Enjoy preparing and savoring this flavorful and comforting French dish, Normandy-style Chicken, which beautifully combines savory chicken with sweet apples and a creamy cider sauce!

Piperade

Ingredients:

- 2 tablespoons olive oil
- 1 onion, thinly sliced
- 1 red bell pepper, thinly sliced
- 1 green bell pepper, thinly sliced
- 1 yellow bell pepper, thinly sliced
- 2 cloves garlic, minced
- 4 ripe tomatoes, peeled, seeded, and chopped (or 1 can (14 oz) diced tomatoes)
- 1/2 teaspoon paprika
- 1/4 teaspoon cayenne pepper (optional, for spice)
- Salt and freshly ground black pepper, to taste
- Fresh basil or parsley, chopped, for garnish (optional)

Instructions:

1. **Prepare the Vegetables:**
   - Heat the olive oil in a large skillet or frying pan over medium heat.
   - Add the thinly sliced onions and sauté until they begin to soften, about 3-4 minutes.
2. **Add the Peppers:**
   - Add the sliced red, green, and yellow bell peppers to the skillet. Sauté for another 8-10 minutes, stirring occasionally, until the peppers are tender and slightly caramelized.
3. **Cook the Tomatoes:**
   - Stir in the minced garlic and cook for 1 minute until fragrant.
   - Add the chopped tomatoes (or canned diced tomatoes) to the skillet. Stir to combine.
4. **Season and Simmer:**
   - Season the mixture with paprika, cayenne pepper (if using), salt, and freshly ground black pepper to taste.
   - Reduce the heat to low and simmer the Piperade for 15-20 minutes, stirring occasionally, until the flavors meld together and the sauce thickens slightly.
5. **Serve:**
   - Serve the Piperade warm as a side dish or as a base for eggs (such as in Basque-style scrambled eggs) or grilled meats.
   - Garnish with chopped fresh basil or parsley if desired.

Tips:

- You can adjust the spiciness of the Piperade by adding more or less cayenne pepper, or omit it altogether if you prefer a milder dish.

- Piperade can be made ahead of time and refrigerated. Reheat gently on the stovetop before serving.
- This versatile dish can also be used as a topping for bruschetta, a filling for omelets, or as a sauce for pasta.

Enjoy making and savoring Piperade, a flavorful and colorful dish that highlights the vibrant vegetables and spices typical of Basque cuisine!

Navarin Printanier

Ingredients:

- 1 1/2 lbs (about 700g) lamb shoulder or stewing lamb, cut into 1-inch cubes
- Salt and freshly ground black pepper, to taste
- 2 tablespoons all-purpose flour
- 2 tablespoons olive oil
- 1 onion, finely chopped
- 2 cloves garlic, minced
- 2 tablespoons tomato paste
- 2 cups (480ml) beef or lamb broth
- 1 cup (240ml) dry white wine
- 1 bay leaf
- 1 sprig fresh thyme
- 4-5 small carrots, peeled and cut into chunks
- 4 small turnips, peeled and cut into chunks
- 8-10 new potatoes, halved or quartered
- 1 cup (150g) fresh or frozen peas
- Chopped fresh parsley, for garnish (optional)

Instructions:

1. **Prepare the Lamb:**
   - Season the lamb cubes with salt and pepper.
   - Dredge the lamb in flour, shaking off any excess.
2. **Brown the Lamb:**
   - In a large Dutch oven or heavy-bottomed pot, heat the olive oil over medium-high heat.
   - Add the lamb cubes in batches and brown them on all sides. Transfer the browned lamb to a plate and set aside.
3. **Cook the Aromatics:**
   - In the same pot, add the chopped onion and cook until softened, about 5 minutes.
   - Add the minced garlic and cook for another minute until fragrant.
4. **Add Tomato Paste and Deglaze:**
   - Stir in the tomato paste and cook for 1-2 minutes to caramelize slightly.
   - Pour in the white wine and scrape up any browned bits from the bottom of the pot.
5. **Simmer the Stew:**
   - Return the browned lamb cubes to the pot.
   - Add the beef or lamb broth, bay leaf, and fresh thyme sprig.
   - Bring the mixture to a simmer, then reduce the heat to low. Cover and simmer gently for about 1 hour, or until the lamb is tender.

6. **Add Vegetables:**
    - Add the carrots, turnips, and new potatoes to the pot.
    - Continue to simmer, covered, for another 20-25 minutes, or until the vegetables are tender and cooked through.
7. **Add Peas and Finish:**
    - Stir in the fresh or frozen peas and cook for an additional 5 minutes, until heated through.
    - Discard the bay leaf and thyme sprig.
    - Adjust seasoning with salt and pepper to taste.
8. **Serve:**
    - Ladle the Navarin Printanier into serving bowls.
    - Garnish with chopped fresh parsley if desired.
    - Serve hot, accompanied by crusty bread or over cooked rice.

Tips:

- Navarin Printanier is traditionally made with spring vegetables, but you can adapt the recipe based on what's in season or available.
- For a thicker stew, you can mash a few pieces of the cooked potatoes against the side of the pot to release their starch and thicken the broth.
- This stew tastes even better the next day as the flavors have more time to meld together. It can be refrigerated for up to 3 days or frozen for longer storage.

Enjoy preparing and savoring this hearty and flavorful French lamb stew, Navarin Printanier, which celebrates the bounty of spring vegetables in a comforting and satisfying dish!

Strawberry Tart

Ingredients:

For the Tart Crust:

- 1 1/4 cups (150g) all-purpose flour
- 1/4 cup (30g) powdered sugar
- 1/4 teaspoon salt
- 1/2 cup (115g) unsalted butter, cold and cut into cubes
- 1 egg yolk
- 1-2 tablespoons cold water, if needed

For the Pastry Cream:

- 1 cup (240ml) whole milk
- 1/2 vanilla bean or 1 teaspoon vanilla extract
- 3 egg yolks
- 1/4 cup (50g) granulated sugar
- 2 tablespoons all-purpose flour
- 2 tablespoons cornstarch

For the Topping:

- 1 pound (450g) fresh strawberries, hulled and halved or quartered
- 1/4 cup apricot jam or preserves, warmed and strained

Instructions:

1. Make the Tart Crust:

- In a food processor, combine the flour, powdered sugar, and salt. Pulse to mix.
- Add the cold butter cubes and pulse until the mixture resembles coarse crumbs.
- Add the egg yolk and pulse again until the dough comes together. If needed, add cold water, 1 tablespoon at a time, until the dough forms a ball.
- Flatten the dough into a disk, wrap it in plastic wrap, and refrigerate for at least 30 minutes.

2. Preheat the Oven:

- Preheat your oven to 375°F (190°C).

3. Roll out and Bake the Tart Crust:

- On a lightly floured surface, roll out the chilled dough into a circle about 12 inches (30 cm) in diameter and 1/4 inch (6 mm) thick.

- Carefully transfer the dough to a 9-inch (23 cm) tart pan with a removable bottom. Press the dough into the bottom and sides of the pan.
- Trim off any excess dough hanging over the edges. Prick the bottom of the crust with a fork.
- Line the crust with parchment paper or foil and fill with pie weights or dried beans.
- Bake the crust in the preheated oven for 15 minutes. Remove the weights and parchment/foil, then bake for an additional 10-12 minutes, or until the crust is golden brown.
- Remove from the oven and let the crust cool completely in the tart pan.

4. Make the Pastry Cream:

- In a saucepan, heat the milk with the vanilla bean (split and scraped) or vanilla extract until just simmering. Remove from heat and let it steep for 10-15 minutes.
- In a bowl, whisk together the egg yolks, sugar, flour, and cornstarch until smooth.
- Gradually pour the warm milk into the egg mixture, whisking constantly.
- Return the mixture to the saucepan and cook over medium heat, stirring constantly with a whisk, until thickened and smooth (about 2-3 minutes).
- Remove from heat, transfer the pastry cream to a bowl, cover with plastic wrap directly on the surface to prevent a skin from forming, and refrigerate until cold.

5. Assemble the Strawberry Tart:

- Once the tart crust and pastry cream are completely cooled, spread the pastry cream evenly into the cooled tart shell.
- Arrange the halved or quartered strawberries in a decorative pattern on top of the pastry cream.

6. Glaze the Tart:

- Warm the apricot jam or preserves in a small saucepan or microwave until liquid.
- Strain the jam through a fine-mesh sieve to remove any fruit pieces or seeds.
- Brush the warm strained jam over the strawberries to create a glossy finish.

7. Serve:

- Chill the tart in the refrigerator for at least 1 hour before serving to allow the flavors to meld.
- Serve slices of the Strawberry Tart chilled. Optionally, garnish with fresh mint leaves.

Tips:

- You can prepare the tart crust and pastry cream ahead of time. Keep the baked crust wrapped in plastic at room temperature and store the pastry cream in the refrigerator. Assemble the tart just before serving.
- Experiment with different arrangements of strawberries for a visually appealing tart.

- The glaze helps to preserve the strawberries and adds shine to the tart. If apricot jam isn't available, you can use other light-colored fruit jams such as peach or apple.

Enjoy creating this elegant and delicious French Strawberry Tart, perfect for showcasing fresh strawberries in a delightful dessert!

www.ingramcontent.com/pod-product-compliance
Lightning Source LLC
LaVergne TN
LVHW081557060526
838201LV00054B/1940